The book is the sort of thing I'd recommend to a foreign language teacher to read curled up by the fire on a rainy day, for meditation, entertainment, and renewal. If I were teaching courses in foreign language education, I'd want all my students to read it as a source of inspiration. I think this book could become a classic.

—John B. Carroll
Kenan Professor of Psychology and Director,
L.L. Thurstone Psychometric Laboratory
University of North Carolina

MEMORY
MEANING
& METHOD

some psychological perspectives on language learning

EARL W. STEVICK

Professor, School of Language Studies
Foreign Service Institute

NEWBURY HOUSE PUBLISHERS, Inc. / Rowley / Massachusetts

Library of Congress Cataloging in Publication Data

Stevick, Earl W
  Memory, meaning & method.

  Bibliography: p.
  1. Language and languages--Study and teaching--
Psychological aspects. 2. Memory. I. Title.
P53.S84   153.1'5   76-2032
ISBN 0-88377-053-9

NEWBURY HOUSE PUBLISHERS, Inc.

Language Science
Language Teaching
Language Learning

68 Middle Road, Rowley, Massachusetts 01969

Printed in the U.S.A.   First printing: April 1976
                                      5 4 3 2

Acknowledgments

The following have read and/or made significant direct contributions to earlier versions of this book:

Marianne Adams, Carol and Nobuo Akiyama, Ann Beusch, Janet Bing, Ray Clark, Laetitia Combrinck, J. R. Frith, R. A. C. Goodison, A. Z. Guiora, John Harvey, Virginia Hodge, Edward and Jean Houghton, A. A. Koski, Edna C. Lennox, Frances Li, Edwin W. Martin, Jr., Peter O'Connell, Sirarpi Ohannessian, Margaret Omar, Ted Plaister, Jennybelle Rardin, Robert Rebert, J. Richard Reid, Elaine Rhymers, Panagiotis Sapountzis, Eileen Scott, James A. Snow, James W. Stone, Lloyd Swift, Dan Tranel, Wm. Van Buskirk, Allen Weinstein; Members of the Psychology Department of Colby College; Russell Campbell and many staff members and students at the American University in Cairo; the students and staff of the Master of Arts Program at the School for International Training, Brattleboro, Vermont, who have listened to me, responded to me, and helped me every autumn for a long time; the staff of the Language Training Mission in Provo, Utah; participants in many staff seminars in the School of Language Studies of the Foreign Service Institute.

Contents

Acknowledgments   v

Preface   xi

PART 1   MEMORY

I Biological Bases for Memory   **3**

Monkeys and Food   4

Rats and Footshock   4

Goldfish, Flatworms, and Others   5

And Catfish   5

Some Ah, Buts   6

II Verbal Memory   **11**

Three Common Aspects of Verbal Learning Experiments   11

Some Relatively Static Aspects of Verbal Memory   12

Some Relatively Dynamic Aspects of Verbal Memory   23

Time   26

"Depth"   30

Conclusion   32

III Memory and the Whole Person   **33**

PART 2   MEANING

IV   Inside the Student: Some Meanings of
     Pronunciation and Fluency   47
     Motivation   48
     Maslow's Hierarchy   49
     Some Meanings of Pronunciation   51
     Some Meanings of Fluency   59
     Conclusion   64

 V   The Meaning of Drills and Exercises   65

VI   Between Teacher and Student:
     The Class as a Small Group   85

PART 3   METHOD

VII A General View of Method   103
     An Autobiographical Statement   104
     The Riddle   104
     An Obiter Dictum on Research   105
     Performance: "Productive" or "Reflective"   107
     Learning: "Defensive" or "Receptive"   109
     A Psychodynamic Interpretation   119
     Conclusion   123

VIII Community Language Learning   125
     A Description of Community Language Learning   126
     Community Language Learning and the
        Principles of Chapter VII   128
     Other Observations on Community Language Learning   132

IX   The Silent Way   135
     Some Basic Facts About the Silent Way   136
     The First Lessons   138
     "Teach, Then Test . . . "   144
     Some General Questions   144
     Conclusion   145

X Some Other Methods   149
   The Saint-Cloud Method   149
   Language Teaching as Applied Linguistics   152
   Audiolingualism   154
   The Work of Georgi Lozanov   155
   Summary: What I Hope For in a Classroom   159

Bibliography   161

Preface

One reader of the manuscript of this book said that "it looks like a report on the literature." That has not been my intent. True, there are frequent references to outside sources. But what I have written here is a personal credo—a statement of beliefs which existed in embryo before I went to the library, but which have become clearer, stronger, and in some respects quite different during four years of reading and experience.

I said in the preface to *Adapting and Writing Language Lessons* (1971) that language study is a "total human experience," and not just an oral-aural or a cognitive one. That intuition was, I believe, a correct one, for which the pages that follow provide documentation and further development.

Earl W. Stevick

Arlington, Virginia
September 30, 1975

MEMORY
MEANING
& METHOD

Part 1. Memory

I

Biological Bases
for Memory

By speech we design great bridges and fight wars, we express our deep feelings and our spiritual aspirations, and even set forth our most subtle linguistic theories. We can talk, we can talk about talk, we can talk about talk about talk, and so on forever. Language is the special treasure of our race. It depends on what we call the mind, but it comes out of the entire person. To learn a second language is to move from one mystery to another.

Because language is ours alone, and language learning is a doubly unique experience, we often talk about it as though it were carried out by minds without bodies. The later chapters of this book will emphasize the ways in which language learning depends on the deeper reaches of the personalities of all those who are involved in the process—on their emotions and their symbolic lives. There, we will deal with those ways in which human beings are most unlike other animals. In this first chapter, however, we shall look at the physical organism which the mind of man uses. We shall not attempt to answer the question "How does the human mind work?" We shall only ask "On the basis of evidence from man and from other species, what seems possible for thinking equipment that is made of flesh and blood?"

MONKEYS AND FOOD

Individual monkeys were placed in an apparatus which limited their freedom of movement. First, they learned that an item of food might appear in either of two windows, and that they could get the food by pressing a lever under the window. In an experiment (Fuster and Alexander 1971), a monkey was shown where the food was, and then a blind was lowered. Between the time when it saw the food (the "cue period") and the time when it was allowed to press the levers, the monkey had to remember where the food was.

Electrodes inserted into the brains of the animals showed that the greatest amount of electrical activity among the prefrontal neurons took place at the transition from the cue period to the delay. On the basis of other research, we also know that this is the same period during which electrical shocks applied to the brain cortex are most likely to disrupt memory (*ibid.* 654 and Gurowitz 1969:6). Other investigators also have noted that electrical activity of the brain changes significantly at the time when a new memory is being consolidated (Hydén 1968:1373).

Inference: At least one part of the physical side of memory is electrical. This is not surprising when we remember that the neurons which bring auditory, visual and other sensory inputs to the brain communicate with one another by means of electrical discharges.

RATS AND FOOTSHOCK

If we put a rat into a compartment with an open door leading into another compartment, we can be sure that before long the rat will explore the second compartment. But suppose that a second or two after the rat sets foot in the second compartment it receives an unpleasant electrical shock to its feet. The next time it is placed in the same apparatus, it will avoid the second compartment. Wandering through the door this time would indicate that, in some sense, the rat had "forgotten" what had happened before. On such a stage, hundreds of rats have played out their parts in dozens of experimental scenarios (*e.g.,* Quartermain *et al.* 1970, Paolino and Levy 1971). A basic finding was that a second shock, strong enough to produce convulsions, might produce exactly this kind of apparently forgetful behavior, or it might not. The important factor was the timing. If the electroconvulsive shock (ECS) came within a very few seconds of the footshock, then the animal would, when next placed in the apparatus, go through the door without hesitation. If the ECS was delayed very long, however, the animal would "remember" to stay in the first compartment.

Inference: The status of the electrical representation of an experience changes very soon after it is formed.

GOLDFISH, FLATWORMS, AND OTHERS

Readers of Sunday supplements and children's encyclopedias are familiar with the so-called "memory-transfer" experiments. In a typical one, goldfish are taught that they can avoid an electrical shock if they will swim to the unlighted end of a test apparatus. Then they are killed and an extract from their brains is injected into other fish. These recipient fish, when tested, are found to swim away from the light significantly more often than similar fish that had received neither training nor injection (Braud 1970).

Inference: Another part of the physical side of memory must be nonelectrical—presumably biochemical. This "memory-transfer" effect is elusive, but apparently real (Gurowitz 1969:76). As a matter of fact, a synthetic substance like that produced in the brains of *rats* that had just learned to avoid the dark had the same effect when injected into *mice* (Malin and Guttman 1972).

AND CATFISH

No one is sure of exactly what kinds of "information" can be passed from animal to animal, or even from species to species, in this way. To call what is transferred "memory" may be misleading (McConnell *et al.* 1970:157). Nevertheless, we do know that when rats are trained to use one paw in preference to another (Hydén and Lange 1968), or when catfish are trained to respond differently to different odors (Rappoport and Daginawala 1968), their brains produce measurable biochemical changes. The biochemical entities involved are various proteins and ribonucleic acids (RNA). The *obvious inference* for a language teacher is that *the technical details of the chemical side of memory lie far outside our direct professional concern.* This is, of course, a correct conclusion. We may still be interested to know that a widely varying list of influences may, under some circumstances, interfere with these chemical processes and so delay or prevent the consolidation of memories. Such influences include barbiturates, anesthetics, and lowered body temperature (Sheer 1970:181).

The physical side of memory, then, seems to have two components. According to a view which has been the basis for much of the research in this field, an original electrochemical pattern is somehow converted into a nonelectrical pattern, which is more durable (Richter 1966:84ff). The process of change to the nonelectrical pattern is subject to interference from electroconvulsive shock, as we have seen. Concussion may have the same effect, as most of us know either from our own experiences or from the experiences of friends. Anoxia and anesthetics may do the same thing. Of more interest to classroom teachers is the fact that even further incoming sensory stimuli may have this effect (*ibid.*).

SOME AH, BUTS

The foregoing picture of how memories are formed is neither hard to understand nor very surprising. It is true as far as it goes, but as stated above it can lead to at least five misleading conclusions. Although language teachers are not given to worrying about base ratios of RNA and never punish students with footshock, these conclusions are closely related to some of the common-sense assumptions that many of us make about the memory process.

Questionable Assumption 1. What you pay attention to you will remember. In other words, attention and memory are parts of a single whole.

But patients who have bilateral surgical lesions in one part of the hippocampal region of the brain demonstrate that this is not necessarily so. They are perfectly normal in intelligence, and they can remember the words and the language skills that they had before the operation. Further, they have no difficulty in hearing, understanding and repeating new information as long as they keep on repeating it. They are different from other people in only one respect: if their repetition of the new material is interrupted in any way, they forget it immediately. Some quite simple material decays in 30 seconds even if there is nothing to distract the patient. Such a patient can even learn a skill, such as tracing a star while looking in a mirror, in a normal way, even though the learning may be spread over several days. But the same patient will have no recollection of having learned it (Milner 1970).

This same body of clinical evidence has already been cited in publications aimed at language specialists (Chafe 1973). Of course we must be cautious in how we interpret such evidence. First, it might be used to infer a distinction and a discontinuity between auditory "short-term memory" and "long-term memory." Some scholars, denying this distinction or minimizing its value, might prefer to say that patients with this lesion are unable to process fully the verbal inputs that they receive after the operation. Still others might attribute the difficulty to recall of certain types of information, rather than to storage of the new memories. Whatever interpretation we choose, however, one fact remains clear: the behavior of these patients is embarrassingly similar to the classroom performance of our students. What these patients have been made surgically *unable* to do, our students often *fail* to do. Awareness, even for a sustained period of time, does not necessarily lead to memory. Nonbiological aspects of this fact will concern us in Chapters II and III.

Questionable Assumption 2. New memories enter the mind the way blueberries fall into a pail. That is to say, memory consolidation takes place instantaneously, or within some very brief period of time, shortly after the sensory input on which it is based.

The experts, however, generally agree that this is not the case. Some memories are evidently consolidated relatively rapidly, and others more slowly (Jarvik 1970:22). Memorization is a dynamic process which continues long after the original event (Russell and Newcombe 1966:21). "Although the protein synthesis which appears to be required for memory occurs during or within minutes after training, inhibition of protein synthesis [by drugs] does not impair memory [in an experiment with mice] for at least three hours after training. This indicates . . . that a different process is utilized for memory storage during this three-hour period [which is unlike the one used for longer-term storage] "—(Barondes and Cohen 1968:457). The time required for all of the biochemical changes to reach completion is uncertain. The total period may be hours, days (Barondes 1970:27), or even months (Deutsch 1971:788). Experimental evidence from Deutsch, cited below, also supports this conclusion.

Questionable Assumption 3. As time passes, memories become weaker at a fairly even rate. This assumption certainly seems to be common sense. But data from an experiment with rats make it seem less certain.

One way of establishing that a subject has some "memory" of something that it has learned is to show that it relearns that item more quickly than it learns comparable material that is new. In this experiment, rats were put into a simple Y-shaped maze. In order to escape from it without receiving a footshock, they had to run to whichever arm of the Y was lighted. At the beginning of the experiment, each animal received only 15 chances. Even after this number of tries, they began to favor the lighted arm of the maze, but they were far from consistent.

In the second stage of the experiment, the rats were allowed as many trials as they needed until they performed correctly on ten consecutive trials, and the total number of trials was recorded. For some rats, the final training began only 30 minutes after the end of the first stage. For other groups it came 1, 3, 5, 7, 10, 14, or 17 days later. Figure 1 shows

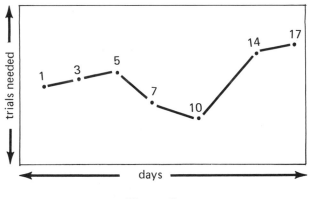

Figure 1

approximately what happened. The rats trained 5 days later needed more trials than those trained after 3 days, and those in turn needed more time than those trained on the first day after the start of the experiment. This much conforms to common-sense expectations. Moreover, if we extend the line from the first to the third to the fifth day and on to the right, the numbers of trials needed on the fourteenth and seventeenth days fall just about where they should. But the number of trials for rats trained on the seventh day was *smaller* than for any of the preceding groups, and for the tenth day it was smaller still (Deutsch 1971:791)! The only independent variable had been the age of the memory.

Again, there is a wide gap between rats running a maze and humans learning to conjugate a verb. Our purpose here is not to say that our students remember better on the seventh and tenth days than on the third or fourteenth. The human memory curve may not have the same general shape as that of Figure 1. We are only questioning the axiomatic status of Assumption 3, not disproving it.

Questionable Assumption 4. Taking in a new memory and bringing back an old one are entirely different processes. The processes are different in many ways, of course, but in at least one interesting way they are equivalent. We have stated that electroconvulsive shock can interfere with a rat's memory of an unpleasant experience. But it has also been discovered, in experiments with the same apparatus, that a rat's apparently "lost" memory can be restored if the rat is put back into the first compartment and then, 1 to 4 hours later *in another site*, is given a "reminder" footshock (Quartermain *et al.* 1970). What is more interesting is that an electroconvulsive shock delivered a few seconds after a "reminding" experience produces the same kind of amnesia that it would produce for the original experience itself (Misanin *et al.* 1968, Schneider and Sherman 1968). Perhaps, then, memory consolidation as a physical process is not entirely a one-way street.

Questionable Assumption 5. You have to remember something before you can revive your emotional reaction to it. This assumption and the evidence against it will be relevant to our discussion of "lathophobic aphasia" (Chapter V). More generally, however—and this is more important—this assumption goes along with the idea of the primacy of the cognitive and intellectual aspects of learning over the affective.

Rats whose overt behavior indicated that they had forgotten a punishing but nonconvulsive footshock were observed to have a rapid heartbeat, indicative of alarm, when they were again placed in the test apparatus (Hine and Paolino 1970). Similarly, a human patient who has had previous electric shock treatments may become upset at the sight of the equipment, even though he may not recall ever having seen it before (Ervin and Andrews 1970:170). Bogoch (1968:25) cites a considerable body of evidence that supports the conclusion that information is rarely, if ever, stored in the human nervous system without affective coding. Schneider *et al.* (1974) argue that the connection between an action and its consequences may be stored in a way that is electrically and chemically quite different from the storage of the connection between the general environment and the same consequence-experience. If this is true, then the recall of affective, "visceral" responses (*ibid.*, 88) has independent standing, and is not a byproduct of conscious recall of details of content. I believe that this question has important, though inconvenient, implications for those of us who prepare materials and teach classes in foreign languages.

* * *

But Blumenthal (1962) was right in saying that neurophysical speculation—and he might have included neurophysical information—is of no immediate relevance for specialists in language training unless it helps to explain and dramatize psychological phenomena. This chapter was intended to contribute toward that purpose.

II

Verbal Memory

THREE COMMON ASPECTS OF
VERBAL LEARNING EXPERIMENTS

Much of our information about verbal memory has come from three general types of experiment. In one type, the subject tries to learn "paired associates": when he hears or sees one member of a pair, he is supposed to provide the other member. One member is almost always a word in the subject's native language. The other member of the pair may also be from the subject's native language, or it may be a picture, or a nonsense group of consonants such as JFG, or something else. This resembles, of course, the foreign language student's learning of vocabulary lists. For this reason, the results of these experiments (see especially pp. 18ff) are of some direct interest to language teachers.

A second very common type of verbal learning experiment exposes the subject to lists of words, always in his native language. The subject is then asked to give the words back in any order, either immediately or after some delay. I know of no comparable experiments using lists that consist entirely of nonsense or foreign language items. Nevertheless, these experiments have cast valuable light on the workings of verbal memory in general, as we shall see below.

In the third type of experiment, the subject is given only one item or group of items and is asked to recall or recognize the entire input, usually after various types of intervening activity. The material used may consist of musical tones (D. Deutsch 1970), pictures, or other things. Most commonly, it consists of words in the subject's native language, or of linguistic nonsense such as trigrams. The first experiment that we will describe falls into this category. It has already been cited a number of times in books and articles aimed at language teachers.

SOME RELATIVELY STATIC
ASPECTS OF VERBAL MEMORY

Memory for Items

Subjects in this experiment (Peterson and Peterson 1959) heard a set of three consonants (*e.g.*, F, B, S), followed immediately by a number. They were then required to count aloud backward by 3's, beginning with that number, until they were asked to give back the three letters that they had heard. When they were required to count backward for only three seconds, their recall was nearly perfect. Longer periods of counting produced more and more mistakes *up to a point*. At about 15 to 18 seconds, the subjects' average accuracy reached a low of about 8% (still better than they could have done by mere chance) *and leveled off there*.

The bend in the curve at about 15 to 18 seconds is one piece of evidence that has been used to support the idea of a qualitative difference, especially for verbal material, between short-term and long-term memories. Of all the findings that have come from research on memory, this is the one that language teachers seem to have heard most about. Carroll in 1966 mentioned that converting short-term memories into long-term memories may be one of the problems of learning, and we shall look at that problem in some detail in Chapter III. Lado (1965, 1971) in a series of studies explored some aspects of the short- vs. long-term memory distinction in the context of foreign language learning. Nevertheless, even this bit of information has received little attention in our profession. Neither Carroll in 1968 nor Jakobovits in 1970, surveying language teaching from a psycholinguistic point of view, mentions the possible applications of research in mnemonics.

If, however, the short-term vs. long-term distinction does have some physical validity, then it has a number of potential uses in the design of teaching methods. It means that after any verbal input to the student's eyes or ears, there is a period of time when this input may remain immediately and unconditionally available for re-examination and for any of a number of kinds of manipulation. Further, it means that the length of this period of time is neither too short nor too long for us to work with in the classroom. In fact, other kinds of evidence support the idea that verbal short-term memory is of about 20 seconds in duration.

Supportive evidence comes very much from the language field, out of the experience of simultaneous interpreters, and also of skilled typists, telegraphers, and court reporters. All these people normally produce their output—typed or spoken words, or dots and dashes—several seconds behind the input that they receive. The length of this delay may amaze the rest of us, but it still does not exceed 20 or 30 seconds. This estimate of the duration of verbal short-term memory is also consistent with the data from the surgical patients described in Chapter I.

A similar picture appears from many of the experiments in which subjects tried to recall, in any order, a list of words that they had heard or seen. The words at the end of such a list are among the ones most likely to be recalled *if the subject is allowed to begin recall immediately.* If there is some interruption, however, this is not the case. The name given to this phenomenon is "the recency effect." The usual explanation for it is that the last few words are still "in short-term memory," while the earlier words in the list have to be retrieved from somewhere else.

If we assume that short-term memory is a dependable phenomenon, then this knowledge is of potential use to language teachers in both directions. It means, on the one hand, that we should not expect our students to remember a new item for very long unless they have done more with it than simply heard it. (We will devote most of Chapter III to some of the things that the student can do to improve retention of new material.)

But the duration of short-term memory also means, in the other direction, that we and our students need not panic when a new item is presented. The item will remain at hand for several seconds if it is not replaced or disturbed during that time by further new inputs. We might, for example, safely allow a few seconds to pass between the time when students first hear a new word and the time when they first repeat it. In free conversation also, or in question-and-answer sessions, teacher and students often seem to operate on the convention that if the student does not immediately understand what is said to him, the teacher should repeat it. But if there really is a short-term memory, then it would also be possible for them to operate by a different convention, under which the student would have a few seconds in which to replay his short-term recording for himself.

The duration of verbal short-term memory should also be of considerable interest to designers of materials to be used with teaching machines.

But the recall of words in a list is not simply a flat curve that rises at the end. As Figure 2 shows, the first few words in such a list are also more likely to be recalled than the words that follow them. Furthermore, this phenomenon, called "the primacy effect," is present whether recall is

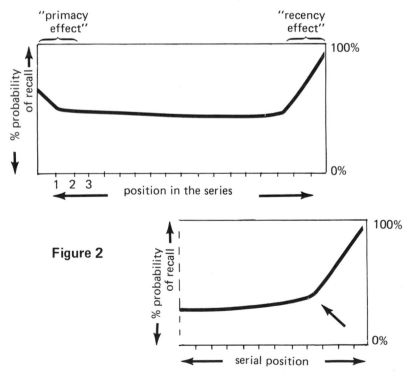

Figure 2

immediate, or whether it is delayed. If the list of words is presented at a slower rate, the number of words at the beginning of the list that benefit from the primacy effect increases, while the number that benefit from the recency effect decreases. The decrease in the recency effect is consistent with the idea of a fixed duration for short-term memory. But what is the meaning of the primacy effect? We will return to this question on page 21.

An interesting variation on the word list experiments was reported by Darley and Murdock (1971). Subjects studied a series of ten 20-word lists. After studying five lists, the subjects were allowed to recall as many words as they could. After studying the other five lists, subjects were required to count forward by 3's—a simple but distracting activity. After the final list, half of the subjects received a final free recall test over all the lists, while the other half were tested for their ability to recognize which of the words had been on the lists.

The main conclusion was that the prior free recall increased quite dramatically the subjects' ability to recall words later on. As language teachers, we may be able to derive from this experiment some helpful suggestions about how we and our students can schedule our study of word lists, and perhaps of other material as well.

Memory for Relationships

What we have said up to this point about verbal memory has applied to memory of individual items. But if any language is to be workable, it must also depend on memory for relationships between items (Reitman 1970:500).

An interesting experiment on the learning of relationships was reported by Reber *et al.* (1967). Subjects in this experiment learned "sentences" that consisted of from 6 to 8 letters chosen from among these five: P, S, T, V, X. The control group in the experiment learned random combinations of these letters. The experimental group learned combinations that were put together according to a set of rules, but the subjects were unaware of this fact.

Both groups made about 17 errors in the first group of 28 sentences and dropped to about 7 errors in the second group. From the third set of sentences on, however, the control group continued to make about 7-9 errors, while the errors of the experimental group dropped steadily and leveled off at about 3. Evidently the experimental group had learned something!

This conclusion was confirmed by a second experiment. After the learning phase described above, the subjects were told that there was a system, but they were *not* told what the system was. They were then asked to judge further strings of letters as conforming to this system, or not conforming to it. As they went along, no one told them whether their judgments were right or wrong. Nevertheless, they turned out to be about 78% right for both conclusions.

This experiment immediately suggests applications to language teaching. Those who have maintained that grammar can be learned through practice of appropriate examples have been proved correct! Needless to say, however, this experiment does not pretend to settle the question of whether that is the most efficient way to learn it. For the purposes of our study of memory, the experiment does at least indicate that relationships, as well as discrete items, can be learned and remembered, even when there is no conscious effort to do so.

"Chunking"

Combinations of items and relationships make possible what have come to be called "chunks." As Miller explained it when he coined the term, a single "chunk" may contain a small or a large amount of information. Nevertheless, short-term memory seems able to span a fairly constant number of chunks, regardless of how much or how little information each contains. For example, the number of unconnected words that we can hold in immediate memory is about the same as the number of unrelated digits, even though a word contains much more information than a digit (Miller 1956).

A striking example of the physiological basis of chunking is found in experiments on recognition of melodies by experienced listeners as contrasted with the performance of naive listeners. It is well known that the dominant hemisphere of the brain is specialized for analytical functions, while the subdominant hemisphere is specialized for holistic processing of experience (Bever and Chiarello, 1974). In these experiments, subjects listened to melodies through one ear, and were later asked to recognize the same melodies or parts of them. The experienced listeners, as expected, performed better. To the point here, however, experienced listeners depend principally on their dominant hemispheres, which were able to perform analysis and chunking; the naive listeners depended on the subdominant hemisphere, which could respond to single notes or to whole melodies, but not to patterns.

Since Miller's original article, a fair amount of research has been devoted to finding out more about "chunks": what they are like, and how many of them short-term memory will hold. In a recent paper on the subject, Simon states his belief that the length of the memory span, measured in chunks, is not constant after all. Moving from one-syllable to three-syllable words, and then to phrases of increasing length, the memory span grows much longer if we measure it in syllables or words, but much shorter if we measure it in chunks (Simon 1974:483). He thinks the number of chunks that can be held in short-term memory for immediate recall is closer to 5 than to 7.

The precise number is not of urgent interest to the language teacher. Nor are we particularly surprised at a relatively constant number of chunks which increase in size as the student gains in experience. Students who on the first day of class are hardly able to reproduce *hasta mañana* are soon able to handle drills that consist of ten-word sentences (Lado 1965:3). What we perhaps sometimes overlook, however are three points: (1) This phenomenon lends itself not only to observation but to deliberate exploitation; (2) the upper limit is much higher than we usually suppose; and (3) chunking is effective over long, though not very short, periods of time (Kleinberg and Kaufman 1971:333). A teacher who has faith in this phenomenon, and who works with it deliberately, can get some amazing results.

One spectacular example of storage of large chunks of information is exhibited in the work of the simultaneous interpreter, to which we have already referred.

Within the classroom, students learning by the Silent Way (Chapter IX) are regularly given silent dictation by a teacher who points rapidly to a series of isolated words on a wall chart. They manage to come back with sentences of incredible length, after only a few hours. The two ingredients that make this performance possible are, presumably, the skillful way in which the teacher builds the chunks up, and the joint faith of teacher and students that the students can do it.

Using a relatively conventional technique of the audiolingual variety, Rassias has succeeded in getting students to memorize prodigious amounts of material in dialog form. Again, the elements of deliberate planning and fervent faith are very much in evidence.

The potential size of chunks appears in a final bit of evidence cited by Simon. Between 20 and 25 chess pieces were placed on a board, and subjects were allowed to look at the arrangement for 5 to 10 seconds. Then they tried to reproduce the arrangement that they had seen. If the pieces had been placed on the board in a purely random fashion, then all subjects tended to get about 6 in the right positions. But if the arrangement had come from an actual game, grandmasters and masters were generally able to reproduce it almost without error. Ordinary players did no better than with the random arrangements. The size of chunks varies dramatically with experience!

Memory for Pairs of Items

Many of the experiments that we have described up to this point have involved memory for lists of items. Another very large body of research has been concerned with pairs of items.

The flashcard, familiar to every language teacher, is a maximally simple example of one of the best-documented principles of memory: things that are stored together tend to be recovered together. This principle is not limited to the two items on opposite sides of a flashcard, however. Many units of information, of many different kinds, are commonly stored in a single, more or less unified "image" (Shiffrin 1970:377). In the very simple case of a word presented visually for memorization, some of this information will include the size and color of the letters, various levels of meaning including the dictionary meaning, its part of speech, and other closely associated words. The image will also include some indication of the time, place, and emotional tone associated with the experience (*ibid.*).

The reader can demonstrate this principle easily by asking someone the last word he or she remembers learning, and then going on to ask when and where it was learned, from whom, what other people were nearby, what the weather was like, where the learner was sitting or standing, and so on.

Anisfeld (1966:113) testifies to the effects of this principle in the language classroom: "A student who studies particular material in one situation . . . may not be able to produce it easily in other situations. Individuals sometimes . . . have greater difficulty in speaking a foreign language in contexts removed from those in which they learned it than in similar ones. Apparently what happens is that during the learning process the new material comes to be connected to many of the cues in the situation . . . Thus every new response [for unimaginative students, at least] appears to be bound by the stimulus context in which it was acquired."

In searching for something in memory, then, we start out with one piece of information, and use it to conjure up one or more images which contain it. We then examine those images until we find the piece of information that we were looking for. In the flashcard example, if the test item is "the blow," we cast about for an image which contains that English expression, plus the circumstance "studying for the German exam," plus something recognizable as a German word. If we are successful, we come up with "der Schlag."

Of course, this is an oversimplification of the way association works in human memory. As we have described "images" in the preceding paragraphs, each one could be like a separate photograph, or phonograph record. In fact, as we know, Item A may bring up an image which contains Items A, B, C, and D. Of these, D may bring up another image consisting of D, E, and F. E may, in turn, bring back still another image, and so on.

This chain of associations may run on freely. One most essential and, at the same time, distinctive feature of human thinking, however, is that we can to some extent assume control of the chain and use it for our own purposes (Atkinson and Shiffrin 1968:90 *et passim*). This is the basis for some useful mnemonic devices, of which we shall look at only two.

Curran (1968:341) suggests the use of "security words" for the study of foreign vocabulary. A "security word" is one example of what psychologists call "mediators." Thus, for associating the meaning of "white" with the Spanish word *blanco,* one might take advantage of the English word "blank," since most blank sheets of paper are white. A slightly more difficult example is the Russian word for "black," pronounced approximately *chorny.* The security word that Curran suggests is "charred." The device may be analyzed as follows:

1.   The conventional flashcard approach would try to associate the Russian sound with the English meaning. But the Russian sound may still bring with it a large number of images, all but one of which are wrong. The strength of these unwanted images may be sufficient to obscure the desired image, like static on a radio program.

2.   One of the many things that may be brought up by *chorny* is the sound [čard].

3. In English, the sound [čard] brings up the meanings "a kind of green leafy vegetable," and "badly scorched but not consumed by fire."

4. A conspicuous part of the second of these two meaning-pictures is "blackness."

5. "Blackness" confirms one of the other images—the correct one—that is generated by *chorny* (step 1).

Note that this chain is a closed one. Note also that it works in more than one direction: without the original association of *chorny* with "black," we would not know which part of the "charred" picture was the relevant one. And if this picture did not contribute to closing the circle, we might use the "green leafy vegetable" picture instead.

In a slightly different technique which follows the same general pattern, the student is given or devises for himself some sort of bizarre image. This image takes the place of the security word. To continue with the same Russian-English example, the student might see a cartoon of a person who had just stood up from scrubbing a floor, and whose knees were black with dirt. The sound of the words "chore" and "knee" leads to the picture, which produces (among other associations) the idea "black," which is confirmed as in the other procedure by the flashcard-type activity of step 1.

The second of these procedures has been used unofficially by language students for generations, and its efficacy has been reported in numerous psychological studies during the past 10 or 15 years. There is evidence that in the learning of paired associates where one or both members of each pair consists of an unfamiliar form, spontaneous use of some kind of mediator is very widespread (Bugelski, 1962). Recently, at least one brief introductory language textbook has been designed around the technique (Groberg 1972), and a group of language teachers have reported an experiment contrasting the results obtained through use of such "interactive imagery" with results obtained in other ways (Ott *et al.* 1973).

The "Worktable" and Subjective Organizing

In these or in other ways, human learners are constantly examining the material that for the moment occupies their short-term memories, selecting appropriate material from long-term memory, and combining the two sets of information. In this respect, short-term memory is something like a worktable on which a person can assemble fragments of information both old and new, take a "picture" (not necessarily visual!) of the new composite image, and file this new image in memory.

There is evidence that a certain amount of subjective organizing goes on in any memorization task, whether the learner has been instructed to do so or not (Tulving 1962). If for some reason the mind is unable to function in these ways while new material is available for processing during short-term memory, future ability to retrieve the material or to recognize it is seriously affected. This has been demonstrated in studies with marijuana (Abel 1971) and with thiopental (Osborn et al. 1967). The drugs had much less effect on the same subjects' ability to retrieve or recognize material that they had learned before the drugs were administered. In the absence of drugs also, there is evidence that for long-term memory tasks but not for short-term ones, people who normally do a large amount of subjective organizing perform better than low subjective organizers. The organizing that they do presumably takes place during the span of short-term memory (Earhard 1970). When a subject is given a list of new items, the first few items undergo more thorough processing of this kind, while processing of the latter items encounters interference from the earlier ones. This must be a large part of the reason for the "primacy effect."

Luria (1968) once wrote a whole book about a man who illustrated this sort of memory functioning to an incredible degree. The man earned a living by giving performances in which he recalled large amounts of data that were presented to him by an audience. These data included word lists, tables of arbitrary numbers, mathematical formulae that he did not understand, and even sentences in foreign languages. It is probably significant that even this man required that there be a few seconds pause between items on a list, and on the other tasks he was of course free to set his own pace in processing the information. He was able to imprint a table of 20 numbers in about 40 seconds, and a table of 50 numbers in 2½ to 3 minutes. If he was required to remember such a table after several months, he needed some time to revive in his mind the entire situation in which he had learned it (recall that material that is stored together is recovered together), but once he had recovered it, he could read from it as fast as he had been able to originally.

This man had another unusual characteristic which was not obviously connected to his phenomenal memory, but which interacted with his memory in an interesting way. He was subject to "synesthesia," in which an input from one sense might register in one or more others. Thus, if someone in the audience happened to cough while he was reading from a table of numbers that he had recalled (*i.e.*, while the image from his long-term storage was laid out on the worktable of his conscious, short-term store), the cough came out not only as a sound, but also as a blob or blur of color over that part of the image that he was looking at, and obscured that number in future attempts to recall it.

His handling of number tables illustrates one of the two basic mechanisms that he used. The other mechanism converted words into visual images of the things they stood for. When he used this mechanism, any failure to recall an item was more a defect of perception than of memory as such. Thus, he once "forgot" from a list the word "pencil." He explained that in his mind he had placed the pencil near a picket fence, where it was hard to see. At another time, the same thing happened to "egg," which he had inadvertently placed in front of a white wall. The next time he had to deal with the word "egg," he made it into a larger image, and saw to it that the place was well lit by putting a street lamp nearby.

It would be a mistake to suppose that this man was just another clever but ordinary person who had become adept at a few parlor tricks. He was apparently born with this ability which, in the long run, proved to be at least as much a curse as a blessing. Nevertheless, all of us use both of his basic mechanisms every day: we store images in their original form (whether visual, auditory, or other); or we bring from long-term memory something that has in the past been associated with the item, and which we think will make our present memory task easier, and then we re-store the item in a new combination. The man Luria described had such a good memory that he was seriously troubled by not being able to forget things, but even this may perhaps be regarded as a tremendous quantitative difference in the number of items per image, rather than as an absolute qualitative difference from other human beings. It is also true that he seemed immune to the effects of "crowding" (see below, p. 29).

SOME RELATIVELY DYNAMIC
ASPECTS OF VERBAL MEMORY

Recall as a Generative Process

Some years ago, in an investigation on the genesis of rumors, Allport showed an individual subject a picture of a group of people on a subway train. He then removed the picture. One by one additional subjects were brought in, and each described to his successor what he knew about the picture. Allport found that, as the story passed from person to person, there was an inexorable tendency for it to change so as to conform to ethnic and other stereotypes that were common to the culture of the subjects.

This demonstration of Allport's makes clear a fundamental fact about how memory operates. In everyday thinking, we assume that to "remember" something is like playing back a tape, even though the tape may have gaps and static on it. The references to memory in the well known book, *I'M OK—YOU'RE OK* (Harris 1967), also use this terminology. But the Allport experiment shows that this view is not wholly adequate.

It is only partially true. In remembering, we do get back some features of the original experience as though from a tape. But another large part of the process consists of generating a new image that contains elements from that "tape," and then recognizing whether that new image is like the original (Deese 1958:219; Martin *et al.* 1968:566; Hogan and Kintsch 1971:565). Judgment about whether the generated image is like the original depends on criteria which already existed within the individual.

This principle helps to illuminate many things that we see in the process of language acquisition. First-language learners, but also adult learners of second languages, when corrected on a matter of grammar, sometimes seem not to have heard the correction. Instead, they respond to the content of what was said.

Someone once took a telephone message for me from a Mr. Feigenbaum. But for this person, the most salient features of the unfamiliar name must have included: (1) German-sounding, (2) first letter is *f*, (3) three syllables with accent on the first, (4) *-gen-* in the middle. The name as written down just moments later was "Flaggenheisch." It had presumably been generated to conform not only to the four facts that we have listed, but also to other facts or criteria already present in the mind of the receiver.

This same phenomenon appears in organized language instruction. I have frequently noticed that students have little or no trouble in producing an acceptable immediate mimicry of the "whistling" /zv/ of Shona. But these same students, asked a few minutes later to produce the same sound from memory or from a written symbol, find it very difficult. In fact, knowledge of the written symbol even seems to interfere with their ability to mimic the sound.

The same seems to be true for English speakers in learning the Swahili word *karíbu* (which means "near"). They have no difficulty at all with it unless and until it reminds them of the English word *caribou*. Once this association has been made, they acquire an almost irresistible urge to put the accent on the first syllable of the Swahili word and to pronounce that syllable with a non-Swahili vowel.

The same students of Swahili provide another dependable example of the same principle. As all language teachers know, *th* in English has two common pronunciations, one as in *thigh* and the other as in *thy*. No English speaker has any difficulty with differentiating this pair of words, either for comprehension or for production. But it is also true in English that the voiced sound as in *thy* occurs almost exclusively in a fixed list of Anglo-Saxon words, some of them very frequent, while *th* spellings in Greek-derived and other unfamiliar words are always pronounced with the unvoiced sound in *thigh*. Swahili has both of these sounds, spelled *th* and *dh*. If we looked only at the phonemic contrasts of English, we would have to predict that the Swahili sounds would cause no confusion for English speakers. In fact, however, many students have an almost ineradicable compulsion to say *nathani* for *nadhani*, and so forth. The recalled part of the pronunciation is "something that in English we would spell *th*." Since both Swahili and English have two sounds for *th*, this criterion is inadequate. The student who is trying to pronounce such a word must therefore supply the missing information from his own inner criteria, one of which is "in unfamiliar words, use the unvoiced sound."

The first hour of work with the Silent Way (Chapter IX) often provides a striking example of the same phenomenon. The student hears a new word such as "rod" only once from the teacher, but produces it many times himself in response to various nonverbal cues. A student may produce such a word successfully 20 or more times at intervals during the first 10 or 15 minutes, and then suddenly appear unable to say it. It is as though, up to that point, he had been copying the word from some sort of sensory store, even though the most recent occurrence of the word may have been as much as half a minute earlier. Suddenly, for some reason, he tries to generate it on the basis of whatever facts he has noticed about it, but these "inner criteria" are not yet adequate for the job.

In studies of memory, then, recall and recognition are for many purposes quite different from one another. In general, the ability to recognize whether one has seen an item before is greater than the ability to retrieve the same item from storage. (Watkins, 1974, describes an experimental situation in which this seems not to have been true.) But, although recognition is relatively powerful, we have seen that its ability to make sufficiently fine discriminations depends on the adequacy of the inner criteria with which it operates.

Effects of Cognitive Activity of the Learner

If the use of associative mediators (p. 19) produces better retention than simple repetition does, it seems to be the case that the quality of the mediators and the student's personal investment in them may also have a powerful effect on memory. In one series of experiments, subjects were given groups of three nouns and required to remember them after 3, 6, or 24 seconds of distracting activity. Some subjects were instructed to read the nouns aloud, while others either counted the letters or labeled each word according to a simple semantic criterion. After 3 or 6 seconds (still within short-term memory), those who had read the words aloud performed better, but after 24 seconds of the intervening activity, they performed as poorly as the others. Later experiments in the same series required that some of the subjects put the nouns into sentences; there were not any very decisive results. But when subjects were told to form one sentence that would contain all three words, retention was 2 or 3 times better than in the preceding experiments (Kintsch et al. 1971).

Another group of investigators (Bower and Winzenz 1970) had subjects learn pairs of unrelated concrete nouns, at the rate of 5 seconds per item. One group of subjects rehearsed each pair silently. A second group read aloud a sentence that contained the nouns. A third group made up their own sentences and said them aloud. The last group visualized a mental picture in which the referents of the two nouns were in some kind of vivid interaction with each other, *but said nothing aloud.* Each of these four groups performed better than the one before it. Bower and Winzenz concluded that "the student's memory benefits from actively searching out, discovering and depicting," as contrasted with rote repetition, sentence reading, or even generation of their own relatively unimaginative sentences. (*ibid.*; cf. also Modigliani and Seamon 1974).

Another study (Glanzer and Meinzer 1967 in Bjork 1970) reached a similar conclusion: subjects were given a series of words at intervals of 3.2 seconds. One group used the time after each new word to repeat it aloud six times. The other group had the time free to think about the word and process it mentally. The performance of the second group was superior.

In any event, and by whatever devices, students are able, through exposure to the learning of previously meaningless linguistic responses to familiar stimulus items, to develop skills which are specifically useful in just this kind of task (Postman *et al.* 1968:783). One of these skills certainly involves the use of mediators, but Postman *et al.* suggest that skills may also include "the adoption of a suitable rate of overt responding," and "efficient distribution of rehearsal time between hard and easy items."

TIME

Timing of learning experiences is among the factors which affect memory.

Time Required for Consolidation of New Memories

We have talked about the widely accepted distinction between short-term and long-term memories. Some writers question either the adequacy or the necessity of this distinction. Ervin and Andrews (1970) suggested, in place of "short-term memory," a "sensory register," which holds raw data for scanning, and a "primary memory" with a small capacity and a duration of about 20 seconds. In place of "long-term memory" they postulate "secondary" and "tertiary" memory. Traces in "secondary memory" are variable in duration, and a given item is forgotten largely as a result of interference from similar kinds of information learned before or after. This stage of memory includes most of the "long-term" phenomena studied in controlled laboratory experiments. Finally, "tertiary" memory is distinguished by its durability and its freedom from interference. But entrance into tertiary memory requires months or even years of elapsed time. On the other hand, retrieval from tertiary memory is faster than from secondary memory.

Chafe (1973) and Curran (1974) also propose distinctions very similar to what Ervin and Andrews meant by "secondary" and "tertiary" memories, except that they do not seem to believe that entry into the latter takes such a long time.

Craik, on the other hand, questions the need for the distinction between short- and long-term memories. His arguments are set forth in the last section of this chapter.

No matter how the memory process is divided, however, as we saw in Chapter I, memorization is a dynamic process which continues long after the original event (Russell and Newcombe 1966:21; Benson and Geschwind 1967:542). Further, not all kinds of input are consolidated at the same rate. In one study, an experimenter presented familiar and unfamiliar material to psychiatric patients just before shock therapy, and tested their retention five hours later. The results of the study suggested that memory traces for familiar types of material consolidated rapidly enough so that they were not disrupted by electroconvulsive shock that was applied a minute later; unfamiliar material was still vulnerable to disruption (Metcalfe 1966:10).

Other scholars believe that what is important and emotionally charged tends to be more rapidly embedded than material which is emotionally neutral or unimportant (Brierly 1966; cf., the role of "salience" in Chafe 1973). This is of interest in the present chapter, but will take on even greater importance in the context of Chapter III.

Probably related to this point is an observation which Miller (1951:218) reported concerning a relationship between memory and sleep. "Where meaningful stories are recalled . . . the details essential to the story are remembered as well after waking activity as after sleep; the irrelevant details are recalled better after sleeping than after the same amount of time spent in wakeful activity." Also, forgetting of nonsense syllables is dependably slower during sleep. The memory traces for what is unfamiliar and only partially understood (*vide supra*) need a longer time without disruption from new inputs. (For a more recent discussion of the effects of sleep on memory, see Fowler *et al.* 1973.) The language teacher will have no difficulty in seeing the relevance of this principle to the study of new vocabulary or the learning of new dialogs.

Spacing

One of the "laws of learning" proposed by some psychologists stated that "the amount learned is a direct function of study time regardless of how that time is distributed" (Underwood 1970:573). A large amount of evidence, however, runs against this law. In studies that contrasted "massed practice" (numerous consecutive exposures to an item) with "distributed practice" (the same number of exposures interspersed among other items), distributed practice consistently proved to be superior. This was true both for free recall of individual items and for the learning of paired associates, comparable to the learning of vocabulary lists in the study of foreign languages. It was also true when subjects tried to learn discrimination between pairs of words one of which was arbitrarily designated as "correct" (Underwood 1969, 1970; Melton 1970; Ciccone 1973). Compare the use of minimal pairs of words in the study of foreign language pronunciation. In addition to better recall, subjects also perceived the distributed items to have occurred more frequently than the massed items (Underwood 1969). Furthermore, the distributed practice effect appeared to persist over much longer time lags than the benefits from massed practice (Melton 1970:604). Some possible applications of these findings in the foreign language classroom are obvious.

Much remains to be learned about the precise mechanics of distributed practice. As the interval between two repetitions of an item is increased, performance improves up to a point and then declines (Bjork 1970). Some writers suggest that the superiority of distributed practice lies in the fact that it allows the mind to store a greater variety of cues instead of storing multiple copies of essentially the same image (Melton 1970; Gartman and Johnson 1972:808). If this is the case, then perhaps the second image supports the first only if the first is recent enough so that it is still readily available. Under these circumstances, having two or more nonadjacent images may help to nullify the effects of "crowding" (p. 29).

Pacing

Even if we eventually learn the answers to some of the questions about spacing of distributed practice, we probably should not use the knowledge to design precisely timed presentation devices for use with all students. Two separate studies point away from any such applications.

In the first, subjects were presented with sequences of 12 letters, one

letter at a time. Memory was considerably better when the subjects were
allowed to move from one letter to the next at their own pace, compared
to seeing the same material presented in the same amount of time but at a
constant rhythm (Pinkus and Laughery 1970).

The second study involved a quite different task, the learning of
paired associates, for which an unannounced retention test was given a
week or two later. One reason advanced by the investigator (Nelson 1971)
to explain unusually high retention in the experiment was that the subjects
were allowed to move through the test at their own pace.

Crowding

One slightly surprising fact about remembering and forgetting was
discovered in the 19th century by Ebbinghaus: If a subject requires 10
trials in order to learn to a given standard a list of 10 items, then in order
to learn equally well a list of 20 comparable items, the same subject will
require 20 trials. Since each trial takes twice as long as a trial of the
10-word list, the total time is *four* times as long to learn *twice* as many
items. To put the same idea in another way, it takes twice as much time to
learn a 20-word list as it takes to learn two 10-word lists. There is a catch,
however. Although tests administered shortly after learning will show that
the lists have been learned equally well, a test administered a week later
will give quite different results. At that time, the subjects who learned the
20-word list will be much better able to recall the material than those who
learned the 10-word lists. The reason, of course, is that they had to learn
the individual items better in the first place (Ceraso 1967).

Suppose, now, that a subject learns two ten-word lists with a given
degree of thoroughness, and that none of the individual items are the
same. To help him in recall a short time later, he will have at hand
whatever coding or processing he did for the items, plus the very
important temporal clue of knowing when he learned each one (Shiffrin
1970:387). With the passage of time, however, this latter difference
between the lists, or among individual items, becomes a smaller and
smaller *percentage of the total period* that has elapsed since the time of
learning. By the end of even one day, the temporal clue will have become
almost useless. This phenomenon is found when the subject is asked to
recall items, but not when he is asked to recognize them or to remember
which items were associated with which other items (Ceraso 1967).

"DEPTH"

A final set of experimental data center around the work of Craik and his associates. Three key concepts which appear in their investigations are "cognitive depth," "Type 1 and Type 2 processing," and "negative recency."

Cognitive Depth

In one experiment, subjects were given a list of single words. About each word they were asked one question, but not all of the questions were alike. There were, in fact, five different questions: (1) "Is there a word present?" (2) Is the word printed in capitals, or in lower-case letters?" (3) "Does it rhyme with _____?" (4) "Is it a member of the _____ category?" (5) "Does it fit into the following sentence?" Each question requires the subject to process the word to a greater "cognitive depth" than the question that precedes it in the list. Craik defines "cognitive depth" in terms of the meaningfulness extracted from the stimulus (Craik 1973:49). In this experiment, *deeper decisions* required some additional time, but they *led to dramatically better performance* both on a recognition task (*ibid.*, p. 58) and on a recall task (*ibid.*, p. 60). Craik believes that when attention is diverted from an item that is in primary memory, "it will be lost from primary memory and will be *forgotten . . . at a rate appropriate to its level of analysis*" (*ibid.*, p. 51) [emphasis added]. This is again reminiscent of Chafe's concept of "salience" (1973:271).

Types of Processing

Building on this concept of "depth," Craik goes on to distinguish two types of processing which may take place while the subject has an item in primary memory. In "Type 1 processing," the subject merely repeats analyses that he has already carried out. In "Type 2 processing," he continues the processing of the stimulus on to a deeper level. Craik cites experimental evidence to support the idea that the latter increases long-term retention, but the former does not (Craik 1973:51-54; see also Craik and Lockhart 1972). In a language-learning situation, Oller (1971) has demonstrated that sentences are easier to learn if the student meets them in a meaningful context. One reason for this may be that the meaningful context permits more complex processing.

What do Craik's conclusions suggest for the student who performs rapid-fire massed mimicry of a repeated spoken model?

Negative Recency

A telling bit of evidence for Craik's position is found in data on the free recall of word lists. His key experiment began like many others: subjects did free recall of word lists, and the probability of recall for each word was plotted against its position in the series. (Compare the graph of Figure 2.) As expected, when recall began immediately the last few words in the list were the most likely to be recalled (a "strong recency effect"). But unlike other such experiments, this one required the subjects to try at the end to recall *all* of the words from *all* of the lists with which the subject had dealt one at a time. This task produced a striking "negative recency effect": the very words which had occurred at the end of the individual lists and which had been strongest in immediate free recall now were least recalled. Craik (1973:55) interpreted this finding as showing that "words originally retrieved from primary memory were not well registered in the long-term store."

Voicing and Retention

In related experiments some subjects were required to pronounce aloud the words in a list while other subjects only read the items silently or heard them spoken by the experimenter. The recall by both groups of subjects was compared. One report concluded that "it appears that *the requirement of active vocalization at presentation interferes with effective coding operations.* Active vocalization may demand more attention ... The effect may not involve just the disruption of rehearsal strategies, but may instead lessen the selective attention capabilities that are necessary for effective encoding in memory. Thus, *the advantages of [hearing the word rather than pronouncing it oneself] are mainly at the longer retention intervals,* when the information in echoic memory has dissipated" (Tell and Ferguson 1974:349) [emphasis added]. Another study presents evidence that "the nonvoiced items in a serial recall task were processed to a deeper level than the voiced items" (Kappel *et al.* 1973:316).

Again, what does this evidence suggest for presentation of new material in foreign language class?

CONCLUSION

The relation between "cognitive depth" and retention has appeared in many of the studies cited in this chapter, even when the term "depth" did not appear in the discussion. This is particularly true of the references cited from Curran, Ott *et al.*, Kintsch *et al.*, Bower and Winzenz, and Ceraso, as well as the investigators cited in the final section on "depth." In Chapter III, we shall remove the qualifier "cognitive" from this concept, and extend the term "depth" to the entire personality of the learner.

III
Memory and the Whole Person

We don't really follow the news that closely. I'll be doing my work, changing Paul junior's diapers or washing the dishes and I'll hear the news, but when the music comes back, I'll suddenly realize that I've been listening to five minutes, five minutes of the news and I haven't heard a single word the man spoke, not a word. If you ask me what he said, I'd have to say nothing, nothing I can remember.

—*Robert Coles,* The Middle Americans

Though a student may repeat over and over the forms of the language, in doing so he may not be using the language. This point has been made by a number of writers, especially during the past ten years. Language use, these writers say, requires communication, and communication means the resolution of uncertainties. A person who says "I think they close at six" in response to the question "What time do the stores close?" is communicating—resolving the questioner's uncertainty—unless the two of them are in a language course reciting a dialog.

33

This position is useful insofar as it forces us to notice what we are and are not doing in a class, and insofar as it suggests ways in which we can do better. That is, it has both a corrective and a heuristic value. Even outside of the classroom, it helps us to understand Paul junior's mother. What was coming over the radio was not just linguistic forms: the announcer's words were, for some listeners, resolving uncertainties about what was going on in the world that day. But Paul junior's mother, immersed (as one might say) in the diapers and the dishes, had no unanswered questions beyond her own neighborhood. This was why there was no communication, and because there was no communication there was no retention.

This view of communication and language use, as we have said, has certain values. There is, however, one rather limited way of interpreting this view which is seriously inadequate, and which may therefore blind us to a—or *the*—central fact about memory and about learning in general. This interpretation assumes (usually tacitly) that information—that which is ''communicated''—consists of facts (including fictional pseudo-facts). Examples are the answerer's name, if the questioner doesn't know it and would actually like to; questions and answers in a game of Twenty Questions; or a statement about the edibility of a persimmon made to someone who is trying to learn to judge such a matter. According to this view, a student who is reciting a memorized dialog in class is not conveying information, hence not communicating and not using language. This is the sense in which the (subphonemic) "distinctions which cumulatively lead to foreign accent are nonfunctional in language use situations" (Seliger *et al.* 1975:20). In restricting attention to the "fact-fict" band of information, this view represents an unfortunately narrow brand of cognitivism, which would allow us to assume a dichotomy between body and mind, or between intellect and emotion.

The Dimension of "Depth"

What this limited brand of cognitivism misses is a whole dimension that runs at right angles to the "fact-fict" continuum. In Chapter II we saw that mental activity on the part of the subject, whether intentional or unintentional, has a powerful effect on memory. Most of this mental activity was primarily "fact-fict." The missing dimension, the subject of this chapter, we shall call "depth." This word is not a part of the standard vocabulary of memory studies, but we shall use it here as we try to put together a coherent picture of memory from the point of view of foreign language learning.

Some examples may clarify what I mean by "depth." A few years ago, I still thought that because we ordinarily perceive language through acoustic and muscular media, language learning was therefore primarily an acoustic and muscular process. At that time, I hit on an idea for improving my fluency in Swahili, a language which I could already speak and understand to some extent. On my cassette tape recorder, I would simply listen to half-hour Swahili news broadcasts, repeating aloud as I listened. That is to say, I would operate as a simultaneous interpreter does, except that I would not change languages. When I put this plan into practice, however, I was disappointed. I was indeed able to repeat along with the tape fairly well, but the experience produced only fatigue, with no perceptible improvement in my Swahili. The words were going into my ear and out my mouth all right, but they were not disturbing anything in between: in the metaphor of "depth," the words were flowing over my mind so fast that they had no time to sink in. They remained instead on the surface, and evaporated almost immediately.

The research findings of Craik, Tell and Ferguson, and Kappel *et al.* (Chapter II) give one set of reasons why I should not have been surprised at the results of my experiment. The narrow-band cognitivists to whom we referred above would of course point out in addition that in my repetition of the announcer's words there was no communication, and only an outward appearance of language use; they would be right. My reason for recounting the story here is only to illustrate one extreme in the depth dimension—the shallow end of it.

What we do in the usual substitution or transformation drill—even the kind which includes no fact-fict communication—requires us to go a little deeper. We must now relate at least a part of the meaning and structure to meanings and structures that are already in our long-term memory and, on this basis, we must produce an appropriate response to each cue.

We could mention a series of usual classroom activities that lie at successively "deeper" levels: retelling a story, verbatim or in one's own words; improvising variations on a memorized dialog; writing an autobiographical statement based on a model. These allow varying amounts of fact-fict communication.

A crucial point on this continuum is found in the work of simultaneous interpreters. Unlike the student who is doing even the most complex drill, these remarkable people must react to the full range of structure and to the full range of lexical meaning, and come out with an equivalent in another language. But any simultaneous interpreter works under one limitation which is essential for understanding this meaning of "depth": he must not allow the content of what he is saying to make any difference to him. If, for example, he interprets a statement that the weather is going to be unusually cold in Minneapolis this week, and if he himself expects to be in Minneapolis the following day and makes a mental note to take along an extra sweather, then his ability to listen and speak at the same time is impaired or disappears entirely. I have interviewed a large number of simultaneous interpreters on this point, and all have readily acknowledged the existence of this boundary, which is apparently rather well defined. Yet although this line lies far "below" the level at which I was "speaking" Swahili along with the tape, it is still true that all normal use of language takes place at levels that lie even deeper. Below this line lie the connections with our plans, with our most important memories, and with our needs. These are not mere fact-fict information. As we shall see in Chapters IV and V, needs are arranged in a complex hierarchy, and include strong emotional or affective elements. The lowest reaches of this dimension are beyond our conscious awareness.

This meaning for "depth" is then not entirely unlike the use of the same word in the phrase "depth psychology." At the same time, it extends Craik's meaning of the word (Chapter II). It also suggests a more adequate interpretation of the oft-repeated statement that foreign language students should "use the language for communication." If "communication" means "making a difference," then a single speech act may communicate on a number of different levels at once. Or the same utterance which on its "fact-fict" surface is totally noncommunicative (e.g., a sentence in a substitution drill) may carry important meanings (i.e., make important differences to speaker and hearers) on deeper levels. The fact that both speaker and hearers may be unaware of these meanings does not alter the truth of this statement. Chapters IV and V are concerned with some of the deeper meanings for students, while Chapter VI deals with possible meanings for the teacher. In this chapter, we shall confine the discussion to relationships that have been demonstrated experimentally between depth and memory.

Total Physical Response

One kind of unmistakable communication takes place when the speaker gets the hearer to commit his long muscles in the way the speaker intended. On the depth scale, this kind of communication may be rather shallow, but it may still have powerful effects on memory. Asher and his collaborators have demonstrated these effects in their use of "Total Physical Response" instruction.

Early experiments with Total Physical Response involved the teaching of a relatively small number of phrases in Japanese (Kunihara and Asher, 1965) or Russian (Asher 1965). The subjects were either children or college students who learned to only comprehend the language, not to speak it. A total of about 30 minutes of training was divided among three training periods. The experimental group carried out commands in the language, beginning with single words and going on to strings of three or four multi-word commands. The control groups listened, and then either (1) watched someone else execute the commands, or (2) heard an English translation of the commands, or (3) read the translations silently.

Not surprisingly, the experimental group had better comprehension immediately after training. More striking, this group's comprehension deteriorated hardly at all after weeks and even months, while the control groups forgot the material rapidly.

A later report (Asher *et al.* 1974:30) suggests that "most linguistic features can be nested into the imperative form, and if the approach is used creatively . . . , high student interest can be maintained for a long-term training program."

Response in General

In Total Physical Response, the learner reacts with his whole body. This may prove to be of a piece with other, less overt kinds of response. Klein (1956:175) observed:

> The perceptual system works as if it picks up a great deal, concerns itself with a little, and acts upon still less . . . Whatever is registered, even though "irrelevant" to conscious intention, may nevertheless persist and retain independent status . . . Such peripheral registrations provide a source of discharge of active, though not dominant, motives, and . . . further, *coordination with fringe motives is perhaps what gives permanence* or persistence to these perceptual registrations, *i.e., creates memory residues.* [emphasis added]

Brierly (1966:34) states that "what is important and emotionally charged tends to be more rapidly embedded than that which is emotionally neutral or unimportant." Similarly, Richter (1966:96) says:

> More than 99% of the sensory information reaching the brain is quickly forgotten. The small fraction selected for retention is not passively recorded, but is grasped as an active process by the living organism because of its apparent relevance to the basic drives, for possible use at some future date.

What these three writers seem to be saying is that what is essential for memory is response by the learner. "Total Physical Response" is one variety of this, superior to styles of teaching which allow the learner to remain minimally responsive and relatively uncommitted (cf., "Lambert's Principle" in Stevick 1971:23).

The Effects of Personal Significance

In 1970, a group of researchers (Lott, Lott and Walsh 1970) varied the usual paired-associate experiment to include a factor of emotional involvement on the part of the subjects. The subjects, given a list of names of public figures, were asked to say whether they liked, disliked, or felt neutral about each one. They then learned meaningless trigrams, which were paired with the names of these people. The trigrams that they learned best were those paired with the names of people that they liked. Next were the ones associated with disliked persons. Least well learned were those that were tied to neutrally regarded figures. This was the case both when the subjects tried to give one member of a pair in reply to the other member, and also in later free response trials.

Another experiment, with a quite different format, produced comparable results. The subjects were undergraduate students of psychology. Before the start of the experiment, subjects had filled out a personality inventory form and had been warned that they would be tested immediately on the ideas contained in a passage to be read to them. In the experiment itself, individual members of the control group were read a short passage describing an unnamed person. Their recall for the same passage was tested again two days later, but without prior warning. The experimental group was treated in exactly the same way, except that each was told that the passage was derived from that individual's own personality inventory and applied to her alone. The passage itself was carefully constructed to contain 12 items that were favorable, 12 that were unfavorable, and 4 that were ambiguous.

The statistically significant results of this experiment showed that the ego-involved group recalled the unfavorable items better than the other group did, both immediately and after 48 hours. After 48 hours they were also superior in recall of the favorable details of the passage. Over the two-day period, the involved group did less forgetting than the control group (Kamano and Drew 1961).

A particularly interesting series of studies have been devoted to a concept called "arousal." In one key experiment, subjects tried to learn paired associates in which one member of each pair was a word, and the other was a number. Some of the words (e.g., money, rape, slut) were emotionally loaded, while others (e.g., white, pond, berry) were emotionally more neutral. Using a device that measures the electrical resistance of the skin, the investigators discovered that the emotionally loaded words produced a large change in skin resistance—certainly one kind of "physical response," even though it is neither total nor conscious. The neutral words produced little or no change in skin resistance. This physical change was therefore used as a conveniently quantifiable manifestation of "arousal."

At some time after the learning trial, subjects were asked to look at the words and give the numbers that belonged with them. Those who attempted the recall immediately after the learning trial did rather well on the pairs which had produced a small change in skin resistance (the low-arousal words), and very poorly on the pairs that contained high-arousal words.

Other subjects tried to perform the same task, not immediately, but 20 minutes after learning. These subjects remembered both types of pair equally well; less well than the immediate recall group for the low-arousal pairs, but better on the high-arousal pairs. For a third group of subjects, whose recall was delayed until 45 minutes after learning, the results were the reverse of what happened with the immediate recall group: recall of the *high*-arousal pairs was about three times as good as recall of the *low*-arousal pairs! (See Figure 3.) Subjects tested after a week showed the same excellent recall for the high-arousal pairs, but no recall for the low-arousal pairs (Kleinsmith and Kaplan 1963). Similar results were obtained where nonsense syllables were used in place of numbers as responses—a task very close to one way of learning foreign language vocabulary. The absence of forgetting over the period of a week is strongly

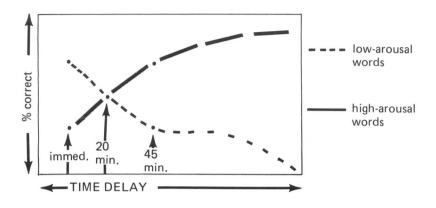

Figure 3

reminiscent of the results obtained in the "Total" Physical Response experiments. The common factor is presence of physical response— muscular and visible in the one series, galvanic and invisible in the other. This is similar to what Curran (1968: *passim*) calls the presence or absence of "self-investment."

A more recent experiment showed similar results when arousal was produced in a different way. Subjects studying an ordinary list were told either that their intelligence was being evaluated, or that the word list itself was. Those in the first group showed poorer retention when tested on the paired associates two minutes after studying them. After 45 minutes, however, their retention was better than that of the other group (Geen 1974). The same investigator had previously reported the same effect for the difference between being observed or unobserved while studying the list, and found that the effect was particularly striking when the two factors were combined.

We might be tempted to conclude that if we want our language students to have good long-term retention, we should make them as nervous as possible while we are presenting new material. This is not necessarily the case, however. Taft (1954), commenting on the effect of this sort of thing on memory, warns that "in some instances, ego involvement tends to raise the defensive process and results in lower recall values, while in others it tends to raise the sensitization process and lead to increased recall." This distinction foreshadows those drawn by Bruner between "defending" and "coping" (1967:129 *et passim*), and by Curran between "defensive" and "receptive" learning (1968:337).

Depth and Memory

It has been demonstrated that stimuli that carry high priority or a strong emotional charge can disrupt memory for stimuli that are presented immediately before or after them (Tulving 1969; Ellis 1971). These are relatively mechanical effects, in which the stronger stimuli in effect prevent their neighbors from getting their proportionate share of time on the "worktable" (p. 21) of short-term memory. The "arousal" phenomena studied by Walker and others, discussed previously, operate in a different and more general way to facilitate or interfere with retention. Bruner (1967:132-133, 147) has suggested that emotions may operate on memory, and on learning in general on a still larger scale and in a way that is different from either of those we have just mentioned:

> When early learning is hemmed about with conflict . . . , it becomes highly charged or libidinized . . . These cognitive structures remain in being into adult life . . . [When learning becomes overly defensive], it finally implicates so much of the patient's world . . . that he is truly crippled.

Rapaport made an even bolder assertion about the relationship between emotions and memory. Emotions do not merely expedite or inhibit memory, he said. They actually provide the principle on which memories are organized (Rapaport 1971:270). Just as Gestalt psychology had shown earlier generalizations about memory to be special cases of its own laws that were stated in terms of meaningfulness and logical organization, so Rapaport hoped for a second revolution, in which "the memory laws based on logical 'meaning' and 'organization' of the memory material refer only to special cases of memory organization; the more general theory of memory is a theory based on 'emotional organization' of memories, *i.e.*, the organization of memories by strivings" (Rapaport 1971:268). The fact that Rapaport's revolution was never realized in the profession as a whole (Luborsky 1971) does not destroy its interest in the light of the other ideas presented in this chapter.

Two recent views of the relationship between depth and memory are found in the work of Curran and of Lozanov. Their conclusions are of particular interest to language teachers because both have developed and tested their theories in actual classes, and not just in controlled experiments of limited scope.

Curran believes that people learn best from utterances in which they have a strong personal stake, or "investment." Partly for this reason, each session includes a certain amount of group conversation. During this time students, with the help of a "knower," say whatever they wish to in the foreign language. These sentences, in the students' own voices, are recorded on tape as the session proceeds. Later, these sentences become the basis for grammatical analysis, manipulative practice, and so forth. These relatively conventional activities gain in effectiveness because the students have felt in their own shared experience the meanings of the sentences, and heard their own voices speaking the sentences from the tape (Curran 1968: Chapter XIV).

Lozanov's work is particulary apropos to a discussion of memory because his method is supposed to produce "hypermnesia": students learn hundreds of words at a session, with little or no forgetting over long periods of time. Because Lozanov's work is little known in many parts of the world, and because it has value for understanding methods other than his own, I shall sketch my own understanding of some of the main outlines of his thought.

Lozanov's view of learning is derived from three observations. (Lozanov would emphasize that they *are* observations based on controlled experiments, and not mere speculations.) The first is that people are able to learn at rates many times greater than what we commonly assume to be the limits of human performance. The second observation is that learning is a "global" event, in the sense that it involves the entire person. The third and most characteristic of Lozanov's observations is that a person is constantly responding to innumerable influences, a few of which are conscious and rational, but most of which are either nonconscious or nonrational or both. The science which Lozanov calls "Suggestology" is concerned with the systematic study of these nonrational and/or nonconscious influences.

But the number and strength of these outside influences requires us to develop at least three kinds of antisuggestive barrier. These barriers are necessary if a human being is to preserve personal identity. They must therefore not be removed. Nevertheless, they may also act to interfere with learning. They do this not only by rejecting new material, but also by preserving the results of previous suggestion, extending back for many years, concerning the limitations on our ability to learn. Lozanov's answer to this impasse is "Suggestopedia." Suggestopedia is the application of suggestological principles, summarized above, to the art of teaching. Lozanov attacks the problem in two directions, and on two planes. The two directions are, first, to "desuggest" the limitations that have resulted from earlier suggestive influences and, second, to suggest various positive ideas. Of the two, Lozanov seems to regard the former as the more important.

The two planes are the conscious and rational plane and the plane of the nonconscious and nonrational. Lozanov emphasizes that inputs on these two planes should support each other, rather than partially cancelling each other. This, in itself, is not a new idea, but Lozanov has apparently made a qualitative leap in the extent of his attention to the details of the relationship between the two planes.

The antisuggestive barriers, then, are to be circumvented and not destroyed. When this has been achieved, the learner reaches a state of what Lozanov's translator calls "infantilisation." (I suspect that the existing English expression "regression in the service of the ego" (Schafer 1958) would mean about the same thing.) In this stage, the learner retains all of his previously acquired knowlege, but becomes more open, plastic, spontaneous and creative. It is in this state that "hypermnesia" becomes possible. Further details about the method itself may be found in Chapter X.

"Depth" and "Communication"

Within the language teaching profession in recent years, we have said and written much about the desirability of "communication" in the classroom. We may evaluate this emphasis in terms of "depth." It is easy enough to devise some kind of communication scale whereon the rote repetition of meaningless material is at the zero point, the giving of meaningful but prescribed responses to stimuli from teacher, tape or textbook is slightly more "communicative," the selection of a situationally appropriate response from among a set of previously practiced responses is still more "communicative," and conversing freely about matters of real and urgent interest is most "communicative" of all. This is reminiscent of the fact-fict dimension discussed earlier in this chapter.

Such a scale would, however, coincide only partially with the dimension of "depth." Much of the difference between the two would be found in the degree of attention given to the same nonconscious and/or nonrational needs that Lozanov has explored. These needs (for teacher as well as for students) may be subtle and submerged, but they are, for all that, no less potent. The surrealistic story which on paper looks asinine may, in the hands of a teacher who understands its use and evidently believes in what he or she is doing, become an instrument for producing astonishing degrees of retention both lexical and structural. The same is true of some of the less "communicative" types of material. On the other hand, talking about real objects or events that have nothing to do with long-term needs, either intellectual or practical, esthetic or social, is notoriously unproductive. My guess is that an increase in "communicativeness" enhances retention and improves pedagogical effectiveness to the extent that it increases the average "depth" of the experience, but only to that extent. We will discuss this subject more fully in Part 2.

Part 2. Meaning

IV
Inside the Student:
Some Meanings of
Pronunciation
and Fluency

In Part 1 of this book, we discussed "memory" in very much the everyday sense of the word. The term "meaning" as the title of this second part, however, is used in a very special and restricted way. It does not refer to dictionary definitions or translation equivalents, or even to the relation of referent to symbol. Rather, it refers to what difference participation in a given activity—drill, dialog or Spanish Club picnic—makes to an individual, relative to his or her entire range of drives and needs. In this chapter and in Chapter V, we shall take a brief look inside the student, to see what some of these forces are, and how they affect language learning. In Chapter VI, we shall take an even briefer look inside the teacher, and then examine some of the forces that are at work among the human beings who gather within the walls of a language classroom.

Some readers may question why this book says so little about "meaning" in the more usual lexical or linguistic sense. After all, we language teachers are now in the midst of a strong revival of interest in this kind of "meaning." Numerous writers emphasize its importance for practice and for classroom communication. How, then, can this book give it so little space?

I see two answers to this question. The first is simply that that is not what this book is about: I am not trying to cover all aspects of language teaching, not even all the important ones. The second answer is that "meaningfulness," in the linguistic sense, has already been treated by many excellent writers, who are too numerous to list here. The personal, psychological, "deep" kind of meaning, on the other hand, has received only passing mention in widely scattered sources. Diller, in private correspondence, has pointed out that a teacher or a method may handle linguistic meaning exquisitely well, and at the same time handle psychological meaning poorly. This book is an attempt to redress the balance.

MOTIVATION

An examination of the student's drives and needs will necessarily include much of what others have already said about "motivation" in language learning. But this latter term has been used on many different levels. Most superficially, it may refer to the desire for a toy, a coin, or a piece of candy which someone has promised as a reward for satisfactory perform-ance. Nearly as shallow, but extending over a longer time span, is the desire for an academic grade. On a slightly deeper plane, fellow language teachers sometimes express envy of the staff of the Foreign Service Institute because our students go directly from training to overseas assignments, and so are highly "motivated." Here also is the student who learns Russian or Japanese in order to be able to read current articles in a professional field. All of these motivations are of the type currently called "instrumental." (Lambert 1963; Jakobovits 1970).

Lying for the most part at deeper levels than "instrumental" motivations are the ones called "integrative." (Lambert 1963; Jakobovits 1970). These include general interest in language study, attitude toward the teacher, attitudes toward the native culture and the foreign culture, and ability to endure being in a position somewhere between them ("anomie"), and the degree to which each student strives for accomplishing the goals that are set before him (Jakobovits 1970:109f). We sometimes catalog together such diverse factors as "tension," adolescent or adult self-consciousness, the individual's unwillingness to violate the solidarity of the group by exceeding its norms, premature satisfaction with partial achievement, and lack of consistent supervisory criticism (Rivers 1968:126). Or, we think of "motivation" in terms of some too-general explanation, such as "drive-reduction," without examining the intervening configurations which determine how such a principle works itself out for specific individuals in specific situations.

The distinction between "instrumental" and "integrative" motivation is a highly useful one, and it would be a mistake to regard these terms as new synonyms for the familiar "extrinsic" and "intrinsic." The desire to prepare oneself for successful consular service in Dakar is, to be sure, both "extrinsic" to language study and also "instrumental"; similarly, the desire to become more like speakers of French, or to identify oneself with the cultural treasures carried by Swahili, may in some sense be called "intrinsic" to the work of learning those languages, and such a desire is certainly "integrative." But what about a "that's right!" from the teacher? Depending on the circumstances and the individuals, that kind of "motivating experience" could be primarily either instrumental or integrative. What about the satisfaction gained from participating success-fully with the teacher or with fellow students in a role-playing exercise? Or if a travel poster contributes almost entirely to the "integrative" type of motivation, is the same true for a set of foreign coins or stamps? My point here is that the instrumental-integrative distinction is not a dichotomy, and also that these two terms cannot readily be paired off with "extrinsic" and "intrinsic."

When we try to understand various motivating events (a grade, a smile, a tinfoil star, a trip to Spain), we should expect them to be psychologically complex, with some features that are "extrinsic" and some that are "intrinsic," some "integrative" and some "instrumental." Moreover, when we are searching for how the events help a student or hinder him, we should look beyond the realm of language itself, or even cross-cultural experience, and try to relate the events to patterns that pervade the entire personality.

MASLOW'S HIERARCHY

In one well known formulation, the needs of human beings appear as a pyramid (Maslow 1970: Chapter 4). At the bottom are the absolute physiological necessities: air, food and water. A person cannot pay attention to or "be motivated by" higher needs until these physiological needs have been taken care of. Next come some less immediate needs which affect security. These include shelter, of course, but they also include stability, protection, and freedom from fear and chaos. When these needs have been tolerably satisfied, the person may shift attention to matters of "belonging": finding one's place in a group, and forming one's own sense of identity consistent with that place. Note that while a person whose security needs have been met may seem to be motivated by unmet needs on the level of "belongingness," the solutions that he has arrived at for the lower-level needs will inevitably restrict the range of available solutions at the higher level. The same principle holds good between any pair of adjacent levels.

Higher still, the person begins to respond to needs for esteem, both from others and from himself. These include the desire for a feeling of strength, independence and adequacy, as well as for reputation, appreciation, and importance to others. Finally, most human of all, but at the same time most fragile, most vulnerable to disruption by unmet needs at other levels, comes the need to realize one's own unique capabilities, to achieve goals that are related to one's own purposes, to see one's life as making sense in a satisfying way. This is something like what Maslow means by "self-actualization," or what Curran means by "redemption."

In most of our foreign language classrooms, we can assume that students (and teacher) have found at least tolerable satisfaction for their physical needs, but we cannot in any of our classrooms assume that students (or teacher) are comfortable either at the level of "identity" or at the level of "self-esteem." Yet, with the exception of a growing amount of attention to "integrative" factors, which lie on the "identity" level, virtually all of our discussions of motivation have been concerned with the top two layers: conscious desires for one or another kind of achievement.

Failure to meet the needs of physical survival results in death or in bodily damage (which in turn may have emotional side effects). Failure to deal successfully with needs for identity and self-esteem results in emotional problems, the side effects of which may be both physical and intellectual.

But the many emotional problems that one person encounters in his lifetime are not unrelated to one another. Rather, they are in some sense examples of one or more of a few general types of problem. Furthermore, individuals encounter examples of each of these types very early in life, and find one or another way of dealing with them. As the months and years pass, people tend to use over and over again the kinds of solution which have proved satisfactory in the past and to which they have become accustomed. The patterns of behavior which arise in this way make up much of the subject matter of psychoanalysis. Early and serious defeats in these areas are major sources of personality disorders (Bruner 1967:132).

There are, then, at least three reasons why teachers and students of foreign languages can profit from a better understanding of what we have called "security," "identification" and "self-esteem." First, in any given situation we need to be able to separate problems that originate on these levels from purely intellectual or linguistic components. Second, if we can recognize these problems, we may be in a better position to deal with them and thereby alleviate them. Their physical and intellectual side-effects will then interfere less with learning. Third, and perhaps least important, we can use partial satisfaction of needs at these levels as very appropriate (and "meaningful," in the sense discussed at the beginning of this chapter) rewards both for engaging in general types of activity (performing a dialog, doing a special project, participating in a routine grammar drill, etc.), and for having learned specific bits of the language.

The personality patterns which a student brings with him to the classroom will affect his behavior there in two principal areas. The area that we tend to think of first is his attitude toward the language itself, both as one more set of academic hurdles, and as something associated with a group of which he is not a member. The second area includes his relationships with other people, particularly with his peers and with those in authority over him. In the remainder of this chapter, we shall make an assumption that is as controversial as it is crucial: what is fixed in the student's personality when he enters class in September is *not* the absolute degree of his ability to hear phonetic distinctions, or of his willingness to relate to things foreign, or of his readiness to work cooperatively with fellow students. What *is* already established is a range *within which* variables such as these can—and inevitably will—fluctuate as time goes on.

SOME MEANINGS OF PRONUNCIATION

What does accuracy of pronunciation "mean" to nonnative speakers— including students—of a language? Much of the evidence that I would like to present in preparing to answer this question will be taken from my own experiences. I recognize that this evidence is anecdotal and largely introspective. Nevertheless, it has the merit of providing contrasting pictures from within a single personality.

We may look at pronunciation in two ways. First, and especially within the tradition that has viewed language teaching as one kind of applied linguistics, we may see it as consisting of control of a number of discrete features that we have called phonemic distinctions. Thus we have often been counselled to aim for a pronunciation that is at least "phonemically accurate" even though the allophones may be noticeably foreign. This is pronunciation with attention to the things that a critic might put his fingers on. We may call this the "analytical" (or "digital") view of pronunciation.

The second point of view takes pronunciation as a continuum. Although no two human voices are identical, the nonnative may produce his utterances, his intonations and rhythms, his vowels and consonants, in ways which are more or less parallel to the patterns that are shared among native speakers. This is a matter of degree, with no sharp dividing lines between correct and incorrect. We shall call this the "holistic" view of pronunciation. I would like to suggest that with respect to the needs and anxieties of students, the "analytical" and "holistic" points of view lead to different results.

Our attitudes toward these two kinds of pronunciation accuracy sometimes find explicit statement. One of my daughters, doing rather well in eighth-grade French, explained to me that she *could* have spoken French so it would sound like the voices on the tape, but she didn't want to sound unacceptable to her classmates. This is an oft-related story in junior high school, but adults sometimes react in the same way. As we reach maturity, we become part of groups of all sizes, some very small and others numbering millions of people (Tiger 1969). We depend on these groups as we establish and maintain our images of ourselves, and as we establish routines which protect us from the ravages of "overchoice" (Toffler 1970:234), and as we provide for our physical and economic security. One natural way of showing to which of these groups we are loyal is through our speech (Labov 1966:487ff), and *particularly through those aspects of speech which are least accessible to conscious choice.* The analytical aspects of pronunciation (the distinction between *u* and *ou* in French, for example) are much more accessible than the "sub-phonemic," nondigital aspects (rhythm, voice quality, precise vowel quality, etc.).

Listeners—including ourselves—from our own in-groups, when they hear us go beyond the gross and digital kind of accuracy, may feel a threat at the level of "identity." This is why, at least during one period of English history, no gentleman who was learning French would "stoop to adopt the effeminate and obviously degenerate way of speaking that is used by the French people" (Rivers 1968:132). To do so would be "integrative" toward a dangerous out-group and *ipso facto* dis-"integrative" toward the in-group. This feeling on the part of listeners is not entirely mistaken: in my own study of foreign languages, even dead ones, I have regularly developed an "integrative" attitude toward the peoples who speak or spoke them. Seliger *et al.* (1975:20) report that among a group of people who had learned a foreign language after puberty, those who learned it without an accent had relatively few close friends who spoke the same first language as they did, compared with those who learned the same new language with an accent.

One body of research on the relationship between pronunciation ability and other aspects of personality made use of a distinction similar to the one that we have drawn between the analytical and holistic points of view. In a crucial part of this research, subjects were taught a few brief dialogs in Japanese. Then they were tested in two ways: first by engaging in a simple conversation with the teacher, and then by repeating after the teacher five simple sentences based on patterns that they had met during the training phase. Competent judges then rated what they had said according to (1) "general authenticity" (comparable to the holistic point of view) and (2) "specific criteria" (comparable to the analytical point of view). Earlier, similar experiments used French as the experimental language. Each student in the Japanese experiment thus received four scores: general authenticity on (1) spontaneous production and (2) repetition, and specific criteria on (3) spontaneous production and (4) repetition. The aim of the researchers was to find statistically reliable correlations among these scores and other measurable characteristics of the subjects.

Not very surprisingly, the strongest relationship was between these scores on the one hand, and the Scholastic Achievement Test—Verbal Ability Scores on the other.

Of considerably greater interest was the strong positive correlation between the "spontaneous specific criteria" scores and the subjects' scores on a test which was devised especially for this research. In that test, a subject watched a motion picture of a patient during a psychiatric interview. The subject was to watch for fleeting changes of facial expression. In one of the experiments, the film was played at successively slower speeds. Subjects differed markedly from one another in their ability to detect these "micro-momentary expressions" (MME's). There was a strong correlation between relative authenticity of pronunciation and relative ability to pick out MME's (Guiora *et al.* 1967). This was particularly true for the specific criteria under the condition of spontaneous production. Note that although the judges were listening "analytically" as they evaluated the specific criteria, the subjects had not been drilled on these points as such. They had thus picked up these isolable features of pronunciation in the course of a largely nonanalytical reaction to the language.

The meaning of this relationship requires some interpretation. The experimenters' purpose in recording the subjects' sensitivity to MME's was to measure their ability to achieve "empathy" with other people. This quality they described as a process of comprehending, in which boundaries between the self and an object outside the self were temporarily weakened. In this way, the subject is able to achieve an "immediate emotional apprehension of another's emotional experience, and then use this experience cognitively to gain some understanding of the other person" (*ibid.*). They assumed that the more sensitive a person is to the feelings and behavior of others, the more likely he is to perceive and recognize the subtleties of a second language and incorporate them into his own speaking (Taylor *et al.* 1971:147). They pointed out that language development and the ability to emphasize came along at about the same time in the life of a child, and that both depend on a warm and close relationship between the child and a mothering person (*ibid.*).

The same authors have developed an even more comprehensive picture of the relationship between pronunciation and personality. In their view, the language ego, like the body ego, has definite outlines and firm boundaries (Guiora 1972a:144). Of the contributions which the language ego makes to total self-representation, pronunciation is the most critical and the most valuable (Guiora 1972a:145). A recent summary of this series of studies is Guiora *et al.* (1975).

But the empathic process may act on the boundaries of the language ego. Guiora defines "empathy" as "a process of comprehending in which a temporary fusion of self-object boundaries, as in the earliest pattern of object relations, permits an immediate emotional apprehension of the affective experience of others, this sensing being used by the cognitive functions to gain understanding of the other" (Guiora 1965:779). This means, among other things, that the empathic process depends on the ability to suspend, if only temporarily and partially, the functions that *maintain one's separateness* from others (Guiora 1972a:148). Because this suspension moves in the direction of an earlier mode of psychic functioning, it is in the psychiatric sense "regressive," but because it is temporary and partial, this regression remains under cognitive control, and in the service of the ego (Guiora *et al.* 1967; cf., Schafer 1958).

Some of the evidence which Guiora and his colleagues have presented shows that "empathy," at least as they have measured it, is in fact one predictor of pronunciation accuracy (Guiora 1970:536, and earlier citations). One factor in the empathy dimension is "tolerance to anxiety caused by awareness of affective stimuli" (*ibid.*). I would suggest that alien pronunciations may be perceived as "affective stimuli."

This is particularly likely for a person who is psychologically very dependent on a monolingual (or even monodialectal!) peer group. Hill (1971) points out that in some cultures, phonation is the focus of much attention as a mark of ethnic, regional or sexual identity, while in others it is much less so. She therefore challenges the assumption that a person who learns a language as an adult never completely gets rid of a foreign accent. I myself have known three people who have learned accent-free American English well after puberty, and one other, a native speaker of educated British English, who did the same thing. Krashen (1973) has cited evidence that the acquisition or nonacquisition of accent-free pronunciation has less to do with brain maturation than with the socialization which takes place at about the time of puberty.

People vary, then, both individually and culturally, with respect to the significance which pronunciation has as a medium for expressing one's self-concept. They also vary with respect to their tolerance for the affective impact of hearing themselves or someone else sound foreign. At least a part of this tolerance seems to depend on events that took place in the earliest parts of their lives (Taylor *et al.* 1971:147; Guiora 1972b:144). The reasoning of Guiora and his colleagues seems to suggest that a combination of these two types of difference may go far toward explaining individual variations in pronunciation ability.

But the boundaries of the factors are set for each individual only in the sense that each individual has a limited range within which he can fluctuate (Guiora 1972a:144). One study experimentally altered that flexibility by "lowering of inhibitions" through the use of alcohol (Guiora 1972a). One finding of this study was that there did, indeed, seem to be an optimal amount of alcohol which significantly improved pronunciation of a foreign language. Presumably, this was an amount which lowered inhibitions (increased tolerance for anxiety over self-image and over alien noises from other people), while not yet interfering with cognitive control. But the same effects which the alcohol seems to have achieved can also be reached by social means. This is where "receptivity" (Chapter VII) and "controlled regression" become urgently important to the teacher and the learner of pronunciation.

Again, if the reasoning of Guiora et al. is correct (and I am ready to believe that it is), then certain kinds of life history may actually predispose one to pronounce foreign languages extraordinarily well. For example, a child who in infancy had "a warm and close relationship with a mothering person" (Taylor et al. 1971:147) but who never achieved full integration into an adolescent peer group, and whose family was oriented toward groups outside the dialect area to which his peers belonged, might have not only the emotional basis for the necessary empathy, but also a definite positive affect attached to the experience of sounding foreign. He might even try, unconsciously, to use his good foreign pronunciation as a means for getting from outsiders the acceptance that was denied him in his own peer group.

The previous paragraph is an extrapolation from the Guiora studies, and must not be taken too seriously. Yet even if it is wrong in detail, it is still an example of an approach to the meaning of pronunciation. I do feel that intelligent awareness of factors such as these will do more to improve the teaching of pronunciation than all the charts, diagrams, and mechanical devices that we have often depended on in the past.

The power of deep emotional attitudes to facilitate or inhibit pronunciation is illustrated in my own speech.

In all modern languages that I have studied, with one exception, my pronunciation has ranged between superior or near-native. (The same cannot be said for my vocabulary or my fluency). Whether this is matched by my ability to empathize, or whether it is a result of general xenophilia, or whether empathy and xenophilia run hand-in-hand, I cannot say. The exception is Swahili, most of whose speakers speak it as a second language with pronunciation influenced by their respective first languages. Having had no fully authentic model to imitate when I was first learning this language, I tried only for digital accuracy; to this day I have no idea how "African" or how "non-African" my pronunciation is.

I can also speak English with fairly authentic foreign accents from some languages, but not from others. I can do this for all but one of the European languages that I have studied, but not for the non-European ones. Four observations, all of which have some intuitive validity for me, are:

1. My native culture has a long-standing and well established joking relationship with its European cousins, but not with the rest of the world.

2. I do not supervise the teaching of European languages, but I have been involved in designing or running instructional programs for all of the non-European ones that I have studied.

3. The non-European languages are spoken in countries that have within recent history been the objects of colonialist activity on the part of more powerful countries.

4. The speakers of the non-European languages from whom I have learned the language were the first or among the first speakers of those languages that I had heard. They were non-anonymous, fully identified individuals.

Two exceptions will aid in evaluating these hypotheses: (a) The European language in which I have good pronunciation but for which I cannot do the corresponding accent in English is the only one that I learned, for the most part, while living in a country where it was spoken. (b) The language for which I can do a rather authentic accent in English, but which I have never studied and cannot speak at all, is one whose speakers resisted for six intensive weeks my best and most scientific efforts to help them improve their English pronunciation.

At least one hypothesis is consistent with all these data: For me, speaking my native language with a foreign accent is a kind of aggressive behavior (often playful) against the group that speaks that way. If I feel that aggression against a particular group would violate my standards of propriety, then I not only will not but cannot imitate their accent.

A final set of data concern my nonforeign accents in English. Like most people, I sometimes try to reproduce words, sentences, and occasionally whole conversations in some of the better-known regional varieties of the language. Doing so, however, is always in the spoken equivalent of quotation marks, and I never carry on serious business in this way. I feel that the meaning of this kind of behavior is comparable to that of my foreign accents and can be accounted for by the same hypotheses.

The set of data that I would like to summarize now will therefore exclude those limited (and probably unauthentic) fragments of other people's speech, and will include only those styles of pronunciation in which I sometimes conduct serious, sustained communication.

I am aware of three such styles in my own speech. The one that I use most often is my own version of what we may call "educated American." The second I call my "down-home" variety. I have heard other people talk of having such distinctions in their speech, but I never gave the matter much thought until a linguistically trained colleague pointed out my own variation between these two styles. Two facts are very clear to me about my "down-home" style. First, I use it only with strangers, in situations where I want to exert as much personal force as possible, or to resist what I perceive as potential or actual hostility. Thus, I never use it with my family, and since it is a rustic dialect which nonnatives might not recognize as different, I do not bother to use it on foreigners. Second, I cannot produce it at will, as I can my foreign accents. It is completely closed to me except when I need it. By contrast, I can speak "educated" at any time. My third nonforeign style of pronunciation consists of my "educated" style modified by various attempts to accommodate to British usage. These accommodations are not consciously chosen, and in fact I am not certain that I welcome them when I hear myself producing them. I use this style only when in the company of a group of British people, as at an international conference. As in the case of my "down-home" style, I have heard a number of other Americans spontaneously describe the same phenomenon in their own speech. What I have described, while it may not be universal, is certainly not rare or idiosyncratic.

There is, then, a sharp difference in "meaning" between my "down-home" and "pseudo-British" styles on the one hand, and the rest of my accents—native and foreign—on the other. "Pseudo-British" is the result of a very strong integrative orientation. "Down-home" is also integrative in the sense that, by using it, I am trying to identify myself with a hardier, more forceful part of society.

In summary, then, the ways in which I can talk fall into three major categories:

1. Pronunciation of foreign languages. Motivation is both integrative and academic. Can be turned off and on at will.

2. Foreign accents, including some regional American. Motivation is playful or aggressive or both. Can be turned on and off at will, but cannot be used for serious communication.

3. "Down-home" and "pseudo-British." Motivation entirely integrative. Cannot be turned on at will. Usable in serious communication.

If this pattern or similar patterns occur in the speech of many other people, then we will be forced to abandon, as too shallow, the kind of exhortation that I, through most of my career, have urged on my students: "Your inability to produce foreign sounds is not physiological, but psychological. Get yourself into the proper frame of mind by pretending that you are making a hilariously funny imitation of the foreign speaker. You may hesitate to do so because you feel it is not polite, but your intentions will be pure, and the results will please the native speaker" (based on Moulton 1966:49). In so advising our students, we have asked them to set one emotion to doing the work of another. Only after I had taught the same phonetics course several times did I begin to realize that it was counterproductive, at least with female students, to tell them that an implosive /g/ was the sound that fifth-grade boys sometimes produced in the back of the classroom to amuse each other and annoy the teacher.

Notice that I have not suggested that most people will display the *same* set of relationships between specific speech styles and specific affective meanings. For the purposes of my argument it will be sufficient if in the speech of most people the affect connected with some variations in pronunciation is qualitatively different from that connected with others.

SOME MEANINGS OF FLUENCY

In our discussion of the meanings of pronunciation, we made repeated references to the effects of the need for *identity:* I must know who I think I am and who I think I am not; seeking or rejecting closer ties with various groups is one way in which I verify and maintain that image of myself; how I use language is one way in which I communicate my desires relative to those groups.

Related to the need for identification with a group, but separable from it, is the need to *interact* with people. Nida (1972:59f) provides, within the field of second-language acquisition, an apt illustration of this distinction. A North American lawyer did much of his work in Latin America, and so had numerous occasions to interact with speakers of Spanish. Accordingly, he developed excellent ability both to read the language and to understand it when it was spoken. He was, however, unable to produce even a decent sentence in Spanish. His pronunciation was execrable, his grammatical control almost nonexistent, and his vocabulary poor. As a result, he always traveled with an interpreter. The interpreter was in Nida's view an important part of the "meaning": a prestige symbol, which served to keep the Latin Americans at a distance and to maintain, as a part of his self-image, the lawyer's sense of superiority.

The need to interact, like the need for identity, figures in the development or inhibition of all aspects of second-language competence, but it is especially conspicuous in relation to fluency. This need makes itself felt at different levels. The "instrumental-integrative" terminology is again useful here: one person may "interact" in order to get what the title of one phrase book calls "all you want in France"; another may do so in order to "transact routine business and participate in specialized discussions within a professional field"; in a language class, students may interact because the free conversation period has arrived and interaction is required for a grade. These are "instrumental" motivations. If we are to be satisfied with the term "integrative" as the other half of a comprehensive classification of motives for using a language, then it must include more than just the student's desire to learn more about an alien cultural community as though he were interested in becoming a potential member of it (Lambert in Jakobovits 1970:62). It must also cover readiness to interact with people in general, and with other occupants of the language classroom in particular.

How ready one is to interact with another depends on what he expects the consequences of the interaction will be. This statement is abstract, dangerously susceptible to tautological self-fulfillment, and is made with no pretense of proof. Nevertheless, it will serve as a peg on which to hang other statements, some of which receive support from research findings.

An individual's expectations of the consequences of an interaction depend, in turn, on two sets of factors. First and deepest is his pre-existing personality structure. As previously stated, the word "structure" in this context refers not to a set of fixed points, but to a set of fixed ranges within which the individual at any given time is free to operate. A "personality structure" includes a self-concept, which is itself complex. This set of factors will be discussed in Chapters V and VI. The second set includes whatever happens in the classroom. This set is not as deep as the first, but it has the advantage of being relatively open to outside intervention. These factors are treated on pp. 76-83, 91-97, 116-119.

Influence of Pre-existing Factors on Interaction

Nida (*ibid.*) gives a striking example of how concerns about identity may influence readiness to interact through the use of language. An Aztec woman who lived in a Spanish-speaking village in Mexico seemed to be able to speak Spanish only when she was drunk, but then she spoke it fluently and with great accuracy. Nida speculates that her failure to speak Spanish while sober was not simply stubbornness; rather, it was at the same time a part of playing her social role of "dumb Indian," and one way of expressing her resentment and her refusal to identify with the dominant culture.

Insistence on using one language with certain people and another language with others is a phenomenon that is commonly observed in bilingual children. It is most acute at the same age (roughly 2 to 3 years) when a child is in the process of forming an image of itself as a person separate from other people. As we grow older, we no longer refuse absolutely to speak "the wrong language" with others, but fluency may be strongly affected by these same considerations.

The fluency requirement may threaten a self-image at other points besides this one. Obviously, other things being equal, a person who sees herself or himself as the "strong silent type" will resist verbal interaction more than someone with an "outgoing, gregarious" self-concept. More important, though less obvious, is the fact that many other threats to a student's ego may result in a withdrawing type of defense mechanism. "I usually succeed at what I try" is threatened by failures small or large; theoretically at least, "I'm no good at languages" might feel temporarily threatened by success. "I'm a professional preparing for an important job" is threatened by materials that seem irrelevant, and "I'm eye-minded" by the withholding of written materials; "I'm a student, and students are supposed to be taught" reacts badly either to a poor teacher or to a good one who is less directive than expected; difficulties arise in a language classroom for those who have no patience with details; for those who must have something to conform to and also for those who bridle at the demands of any authority.

Any of these threats to a student's ego will produce some kind of adaptive reaction, many of which are of a defensive nature. Some defensive reactions are aggressive, while others consist of some form of withdrawal, and the latter generally bring partial (or occasionally complete) loss of fluency. It would be interesting to notice which students habitually direct inward their annoyance at having made a mistake (apologizing, slapping forehead, muttering "stupid!" etc.) and which ones customarily direct it outward ("dammit," manipulation of objects, etc.), and to see how these two patterns correlate with overall fluency.

Unfortunately, there is no way to dissolve all of the frustrations and potential ego-threats; there is not even a single, magical formula to minimize them. Nevertheless, there is one fundamental change in our approach that might improve our chances of dealing successfully with problems of this kind: During most of my years in language teaching, I have focussed my attention on the linguistic material—the sounds, the words and the structures—that my students were learning. Their emotional reactions, the relationships between what they were experiencing and how it made them feel, were at the periphery of my thinking. I was conscious of those matters only when a student showed gross and overt signs of being upset. Recently, however, I have tried to reverse my priorities. Student attitudes now take chronological priority. This means that I no longer care how much of the language they learn during the first week. Although I do not tell them so, the linguistic material presented during that time is only a vehicle for getting acquainted and for finding and reducing anxieties. Even during the remainder of the course, the first question is "*How* are they learning?" and the second is "*What* have they learned?" It is now content, and not morale, that I tend to ignore unless it threatens to cause trouble. Needless to say, I still give much attention to content; what has changed is the focus.

But threats exist at the level of interaction as well as at the level of identity. One experimenter measured the fluency, rate and total verbal output of a series of subjects who thought they were addressing an ordinary audience. Actually the audience was primed by the experimenter to react in one of two ways. In the first mode, various members of the audience manifested positive kinds of behavior, including smiling, maintaining eye contact, sitting in a comfortable but erect posture, note-taking, and absence of fidgeting. With other speakers, the same audience fidgeted, withheld eye contact, looked around the room, and doodled. The difference between these two modes of audience response produced the expected differences in fluency, rate, and total output, although these effects were not always statistically significant (Blubaugh 1969). If these variations in hearer response can produce this sort of effect in subjects who are speaking their native language, we should not be surprised to find stronger effects on people who are trying to speak a foreign one.

A different pair of experiments in the same general area produced statistically significant results. In both, the dependent variable was not total output or general fluency; rather, it was a number called the "type-token ratio" (TTR). This is the ratio between the total number of words used and the total number of *different* words used.

In the first experiment of this series, the control subjects were simply asked to tell two familiar folk stories selected by the experimenter. The experimental subjects told the same two stories. After the first story, however, they were required to count backward from 15 to 1, alternately subtracting 3 and 4. As they attempted this fairly difficult task, the experimenter interrupted them frequently, showed contempt or irritation when they made errors, and was generally unpleasant. After this aggressive behavior on the part of the experimenter, the subjects went on to tell the second story. Not surprisingly, their TTR's were down. Apparently, in response to a threat, they had "reduced their perimeter" by sticking to a leaner vocabulary than they would otherwise have used.

In a related experiment, the subjects were invited to the experimenter's home and, in the course of the visit, they were asked why they had chosen psychology as their major field of study. The control subjects were allowed to answer freely, while the experimental subjects were criticized, interrupted and misunderstood. As in the previous experiment, the second group showed a drop in TTR. In this informal setting, the difference between groups was even greater (Höweler 1972).

CONCLUSION

Some linguists regard speech as the only certain reality of language—as the physical data which are to be sorted and summarized. They take it for granted that the informant will always speak. Language teachers who are influenced by these linguists are likely to insist that their students do large amounts of oral work, whether mimicry or memorization or something else. Other linguists view speech as only the most superficial manifestation of the interaction of underlying entities and rules. Their counterparts in the field of language teaching may place less emphasis on oral work, and more on mental activity. But they usually trace the origins of speech only as far—only as deep—as their own farthest and deepest understanding of the linguistic structures involved.

In this chapter, we have reminded ourselves that the very utterance of words, regardless of how well or how poorly they are pronounced, depends on sources far beyond the linguistic level. And we have seen that the subtlest details of pronunciation, though they are the most superficial part of language from the point of view of the linguistic analyst, perhaps run deeper into the center of the student's personality than any other aspect of language.

V
The Meaning of
Drills and Exercises

In the preceding chapter, we looked into the meanings of student pronunciation, which is an expression in the physical substance of the language of how the individual responds to its alienness. In this chapter we shall explore the meaning of some classroom activities whose form is under the direct control of the teacher. Classroom activities come in countless sizes and shapes, but the ones that we shall examine most thoroughly are drills and exercises. Chosen because they come nearest to being ubiquitous and inevitable, they illustrate points that can also be made about many of the more specialized forms of classroom activity.

At the Foreign Service Institute of the Department of State, we have customarily distinguished between *drills* and *exercises*. In a drill, there is at any time only one student response that will be accepted as entirely satisfactory, while an exercise may have two or more acceptable answers. Two common types of drill are mimicry-memorization of dialogs, and substitution series in which substitution of a cue word in one sentence produces the next sentence, which, in its turn, is altered in response to a further cue.

The theoretical framework that has been most helpful to me in understanding the meaning of drills has been Transactional Analysis. This view of personality has the incidental advantage of being easily available in relatively readable form (Berne 1964, 1972; Harris 1968) and of having received widespread discussion in recent years. Thus, though I may be spared the task of fully describing the theory, it is necessary to summarize parts of it which are essential for following the argument of this chapter. For that purpose, the most important points may be grouped under three headings: "ego states," "transactions," and "structuring of time." A harmonizing, but different and insightful discussion of drill is provided by Curran (1968:342-351).

Ego States

We have all had occasion, in observing ourselves and others, to see a person's behavior change suddenly. The same biological individual who at one moment was poised and analytical suddenly becomes agitated and begins to talk rapidly, on the verge of tears. Or the person who has been acting in the impatient and selfish manner of a small child may before our very eyes suddenly become self-righteous, critical and dogmatic. Inside the same bone structure, skin and clothes, a number of distinct and coherent systems of feeling seem to co-exist and make themselves visible as distinct and coherent behavior patterns (Harris 1968:38f; Berne 1964:23). In Transactional Analysis, each of these patterns is called an *ego state.*

A fundamental assertion of Transactional Analysis is that the number of ego states within any individual is three—no more and no fewer—and that these ego states are not mere theoretical constructs, but psychological realities (Berne 1964:23). They originate in different aspects, depend on different sets of memory recordings, and produce different results according to which of them is in control at a given moment. Their names (always spelled with a capital letter) are *Parent, Adult* and *Child.*

The Parent. The Parent ego state draws on early memories of how things were in the great, overwhelming world outside the skin of a very young child. Since the child's mother and father (or their substitutes) were by far the most powerful figures in that world, the ego state derives its name from them, but includes data from any other source of the experiences that were imposed on the small child from without. It includes the rules that were taught to the child, but also the ways of living that he saw and heard around him (Harris 1968:41f). These "memory-tapes" cannot be erased, and they influence the individual throughout his entire life.

Numerous clues indicate the moments when a person is probably under the control of his Parent ego state. Some nonverbal clues are a furrowed brow, a pointing index finger, a "horrified" or disapproving look, sighing, and patting another person on the head. Some verbal cues are "always" and "never," which are consistent with a long-standing system of conclusions which are not open to new data; evaluative words, both favorable and unfavorable; "if I were you . . ."; "should" and "ought" (Harris 1968:90). In addition, a person in this ego state is likely to use a tone of voice, gestures and specific facial expressions that he learned many years ago from his own parents.

Being in the Parent ego state is not to be confused with being a biological parent. The ego state manifests itself in very early years, as when small children play "house," or when one tells another "You're not *supposed* to do it that way!" Some popular fictional examples of parents who are also full-time Parents are found in Daniel Greenburg's *How to Be a Jewish Mother* (1964) ("You don't have to be either Jewish or a mother to be a Jewish mother") and the comic strip *Momma.*

Although the Parent ego state is much maligned and often overused, it has certain legitimate and essential functions. To the extent that its data are consistent with present reality, it is useful in controlling and protecting the Child, and in saving the Adult from overwork (Harris 1968:57).

In our analysis of the activities that accompany a language drill, we will find it useful to distinguish between the "natural" or "nurturing" functions of parents and the Parent, and their "controlling" or "bossy" functions (Berne 1972:13). There can, of course, be no sharp line between them, but we will refer to this difference in subsequent chapters.

The Child. The Child ego state comes out of memories about how we thought and acted before approximately age 5, and particularly how we felt (Berne 1972:12; Harris 1968:50, 47). Much of the Child consists of recordings of internal events, some of which were emotional responses to the same external events that became parts of the Parent. By the time a biological child leaves for school, "it is hard to imagine that any emotion exists which (he) has not already felt" (Harris 1968:50). The Child recordings, like the Parent recordings, are unerasable.

There are numerous signs that the Child has been activated. Display of emotion, either pleasant or unpleasant, is one of them (Harris 1968:118). Some specific nonverbal signs, in American culture at least, are rolling eyes, shrugging shoulders, downcast eyes, and raising the hand for permission to speak. Verbally, where the Parent makes sweeping and judgmental statements, the Child is likely to emphasize his lack of responsibility by using such words as "I wish" and "I dunno." He is interested in comparisons, and particularly in establishing that "Mine is Better" than anybody else's. When he wants something, he has no patience with delay, but wants it *now!* (Harris 1968:91).

Much of the energy of the Parent, as we have seen, is spent in protecting and controlling the Child, and the Adult devotes much of its time to getting things that the Child wants. Nevertheless, the Child is much more than a nuisance. Berne tells us that it is "in many ways the most valuable part of the personality" (1964:25), for in the Child reside "intuition, creativity and spontaneous drive and enjoyment" (1964:27). These, of course, are the very qualities that make for language learning that is both "receptive" and "productive" as I have used these terms.

Just as we have distinguished between the Natural and the Controlling Parent, we need to differentiate among the Natural, the Adapted, and the Rebellious Child (Berne 1972:13), and particularly between the first two of these. The Natural Child is self-expressive; the Adapted Child seeks to avoid trouble with the outside power structure, and to get what it wants (1972:104), whether by whining, by compliance, or by dissimulation. The Natural Child is the one that learns languages; the compliant variety of Adapted Child works for good marks.

An important part of the Child recordings in the memory of virtually everyone consists of feelings of inadequacy, of having been wrong, and of having been the object of disapproval, correction and punishment. Given the immaturity and the dependence of the baby, a certain number of these feelings are inevitable. At the time when the infant experiences these feelings, however, he cannot understand the inevitability of his inadequacies and errors. Instead, he accepts these experiences as evidence about himself. This becomes the basis for an "I'm not OK" position which the individual may spend his life expressing, affirming and trying to escape from.

The Adult. Transactional Analysis applies the term Adult to the ego state in which a person "appraises his environment objectively, and calculates its possibilities and probabilities on the basis of past experience'' (Berne 1972:11). This is the Self as it reaches out and tries to make sense of the outside world. This ego state begins at least as soon as an infant is able to move itself around, so that it must begin to choose among alternatives; Gattegno (1973) thinks that it begins at the moment of conception. The incessant asking of questions, so typical of young children, is a striking manifestation of the Adult, and not of the Child. The Adult sometimes is compared to a computer. It reconciles what the Child wants with what the Parent will allow; it then figures out whether the result is advisable under present circumstances and, if so, how to achieve it. Some indications that the Adult is in charge are alert movement of eyes, face and body; questions like *who?*, *what?*, *why?*; expressions like "probably" and "in my opinion," instead of dogmatic statements (Harris 1968:92).

All three ego states are necessary to a healthy personality. What is difficult is to keep them in proper balance with one another, and this task too is grist for the Adult's computer. The Adult, unfortunately, also is the ego state most likely to be swept aside by the others under pressure of external events.

Transactions

In Transactional Analysis, the basic unit of human interaction is called a *stroke*. A stroke is any action that implies recognition of another person's existence. There are good and bad strokes, pleasant and unpleasant ones, and bigger or smaller ones. People differ in their needs for stroking, but even bad strokes are less destructive than stroke-deprivation.

An exchange of strokes is a *transaction*. Depending on the ego states of persons involved, a transaction may be "Parent-Parent," "Parent-Child," "Adult-Adult," etc. Sometimes, two participants have different views of the same transaction. One may try in an Adult ego state to address the other person's Adult, while the second may try to play Parent to the other's Child. Transactions like this, called *crossed transactions*, generally prevent satisfactory communication between the people involved.

Finally, and very important for an understanding of what goes on in a classroom are *ulterior transactions*. Here, what on a social level seems to be, for example, Adult-Adult, on a psychological level is something else, perhaps Child-Child or Parent-Child. Examples of ulterior transactions, as well as a description of six "ways of structuring time," will be found in the following discussion of drills and exercises.

Structuring of Time

What is a drill, in the terminology of Transactional Analysis?

Berne, Harris, and others speak of six ways of structuring time: withdrawal, rituals, activities, pastimes, games, and intimacy. Clearly, a drill does not allow for withdrawal, at least not of the physical kind. It may, however, partake of some of the characteristics of other modes of time-structuring.

Most obviously, a drill is "a socially programmed use of time where everybody agrees to do the same thing" (Harris 1968:143). In this respect, it meets the definition of a ritual. Of rituals we are told that they can keep people apart; that they are designed to get a group of individuals through the hour without anyone having to get close to anyone else; that they require little commitment, and so bring little fulfillment. Insofar as a drill is a ritual, these are warnings to any language teacher who is interested in the psychodynamic aspects of what goes on in class. They are only warnings, however, and not prohibitions; if we use drills, we need to be aware of their possible limitations.

These limitations are, in fact, not necessarily bad. Their very impersonality may at times be exploited as a temporary means of reducing the level of threat and anxiety.

But a drill may also be "a common, convenient, comfortable, and utilitarian method of structuring time by a project designed to deal with the material of external reality." Even though drills are not always comfortable, and even though their actual utility in dealing with the external realities of an alien grammatical system is seriously questioned by many these days, drills probably fit into this, Berne's definition of an "activity." Activities are, externally at least, transactions between the Adult ego states of two or more people (Berne 1972:23). Insofar as they do achieve their stated purpose of making it easier for the student to use correctly some part of the language—or insofar as the student has faith that this is happening!—drills may be highly satisfying in and of themselves (Harris 1968:143). They may also lead to future satisfactions in the form of "stroking for a job well done" (Harris 1968:144)—passing grades, the

Wilder Prize in German, cash rewards from Father, and so on. But again, while an activity is going on, there may or may not be intimate involvement among the participants (Harris 1968:144). Activities, like withdrawal and rituals, can keep people apart. They are consistent with either the presence or the absence of a high level of mutual trust within the classroom. They may or may not form part of an overall pattern that includes significant and mutually edifying communication.

Drills, in the narrow sense in which I use the term here, do not fit into the definition of a "pastime," which will concern us in our discussion of exercises (p. 81ff). In themselves, drills certainly do not qualify as "games." Nevertheless, they can and often do form counters in some of the games that teachers and students play. Or, to change the figure of speech, they may become the fields, or the boards, on which these games are played. Therefore it is necessary to look briefly at "games" as this term is used in Transactional Analysis.

Berne has provided at least two definitions of *game*. The second does not contradict the first, but it does impose additional conditions on use of the term.

(1) Berne (1964:48) said that games differ in two respects from other ways of structuring time. The first difference is that in a game, things happen simultaneously on at least two levels at once. What on the surface seems to be a series of transactions between two Adults turns out to be also, and in a more important way, an exchange between Parent and Child, or between two Child ego states. Berne calls this the "ulterior" quality of games. The second distinguishing characteristic of games, in the 1964 definition, is that each leads to its characteristic "payoff" in the form of feelings (not necessarily identical) which come to each participant or "player."

An example may help to clarify the meaning of this definition of "game." A popular game described by Berne is one that he calls "Why Don't You—Yes But." In this game, the player who is "it" poses a problem to one or more other players and asks for advice. If they agree to play (*i.e.,* if they respond with helpful suggestions), "it" systematically rejects everything they offer. On the social level, this episode was an Adult request for the help of other Adults in dealing with some aspect of external reality. On the psychological level, however, *where the game originated and where the payoffs were felt*, it was something quite different. The Child ego state of "it" was interacting with the Parents in the other players. The "payoff" for "it" is the silence at the end of the game, which shows that the Parents have racked their brains without being able to come up with a satisfactory solution (Berne 1964:120). It is they, and not the Child, who are inadequate. "It's" Child thus gains temporary relief from his NOT-OK position. Payoffs for the other players may take the form of frustration and/or a confirmation of the position that "Children are always ungrateful, and there's no helping them."

The game of "Why Don't You—Yes But" illustrates the ulterior nature of games (the disparity between social and psychological levels), and gives examples of what is meant by "payoffs."

(2) In his later definition of *game* (1972:23), Berne adds the requirement that during the course of the game, there be a "switch" when a response which one player has given for a particular purpose on a particular level is taken by another player and converted to another purpose on another level. There ensues a period of confusion while the first player tries to figure out what has happened, and this in turn is followed by the payoff(s). While this chronological sequence may be a valid inference from the accumulated experience of transactional analysts, this feature does not show up clearly in all of the games which are described in the books on which I have drawn for this chapter. In addition, my purposes here are less comprehensive than those of the therapist. For these two reasons, I shall work principally with Berne's 1964 definition.

Many experienced language teachers to whom I have described "Why Don't You—Yes But" immediately recognize it as one that some of their students have played with them. In the Language Study version, of course, drills and other activities provided by the teacher take the place of the suggestions of helpful friends, but the response of "it" is still to find fault with everything.

It may be that the language teacher who goes from workshop to workshop without finding anything of value, or who rejects as worthless the two or three dozen books currently in print for his language, is himself playing another version of the same game. What is significant here is not the rejection itself, because that may be done for Adult as well as for Child reasons. It is rather the satisfaction at having been able to reject, for this can block out the Adult's capacity to reason and to estimate probabilities.

If, as Transactional Analysis would have us believe, the underlying cause of this kind of behavior is in the "I'M NOT-OK" position which is shared by almost all human beings, then the cure for the behavior does not lie either in reasoning with the person, or in scolding him, or in giving him bad grades. Nor does it lie primarily in designing better, more appropriate drills (or, in the case of the teacher-player, better workshops or more adequate textbooks). It lies rather in finding other ways in which the student can gain relief from his NOT-OK position. Ideally, of course, a student could be helped to move away from that position altogether, and into the position that says "I'M OK." The complete attainment of this goal usually is beyond the scope of the language teacher (and often of the professional therapist as well), but this fact does not alter its appropriateness as a goal, or as a direction to take.

But drills may be the occasion for a number of other games, or at least ulterior transactions, in the language classroom. One of these is what Berne calls "Schlemiel," in which the principal player behaves in ways which are at the same time clumsy and destructive, such as spilling gravy on the host's new rug. This game stems from the same NOT-OK position as "Why Don't You—Yes But," but its aim is to get forgiveness from the opposing player. The central player wins either way, however, for if the opposing player reacts with anger rather than absolution to his spilling gravy on the rug, he can feel justified in returning the resentment. The opponent has shown that *he* is NOT-OK, either!

In a language class, among adult students at least, this kind of game is less likely to involve physical clumsiness, partly because the customary sedentary posture of the students removes most of the opportunities for it. But one cannot help wondering whether the student who persists in both gross and senseless errors which his classmates have long since abandoned is not engaged in the same psychodynamic ploy. I once had a student who uttered the words "I'm sorry" after virtually every one of his fairly numerous mistakes. The first reaction of the staff was to pity and forgive, but soon we became annoyed and even unsettled.

This is not to say that all students who persist in errors we think they should have outgrown are necessarily playing "Schlemiel," any more than all who reject our advice, or find our drills inappropriate, are engaged in a game of "Why Don't You—Yes But." It is the consistent pattern rather than the isolated incident that betrays the game. Nevertheless,

"Schlemiel" is one more example of the psychodynamic maneuvering for which an innocent grammar drill or dialog-memorization assignment may become the vehicle.

A teacher who has detected an ongoing game of "Schlemiel" will be interested in the response which Berne suggests as the most constructive. He suggests that the prospective opponent refuse to play the game at all, whether by responding with anger or by granting forgiveness. Instead, the Adult of the chosen opponent remains in the realm of objective reality, and offers a statement of (how he, at least, sees) that reality. In Berne's example, "Tonight you can embarrass my wife, ruin the furniture and wreck the rug, but please don't say 'I'm sorry' "! He points out, however, that people who initiate this game are often quite intense about it, and that "playing anti-Schlemiel" is not without its dangers.

One game that is probably more common in the language classroom than "Schlemiel" is "Stupid." As in the case of the former, one manifestation of "Stupid" may be the making of mistakes. In this game, however, the goal is not forgiveness. In fact, forgiveness can, for a player of "Stupid," be quite upsetting. What he wants, instead, is for the victim (chosen opponent) in the game to do something that will indicate agreement with his position "I am stupid." That something may consist of words, of course, but it may also consist of a tone of voice used in correction, or of a smile that carries condescension ("What else should I have expected from *you*?"), or it may consist of an impatiently jiggling foot. As for "Schlemiel," Berne's recommended "antithesis" is that the second person simply refuse to play. But because the verbal and nonverbal ways of agreeing with a person's suggestion that he is stupid are so numerous, it is very hard to avoid being drawn into the game unless one's own basic position is, in the words of the book title, that "I'm OK and you're OK."

A successful game of "Stupid" is useful to the student whose preferred reaction to his NOT-OK position is one of withdrawal. When we assent to that position, we are excusing him from the need to study or to learn (Berne 1964:158). "He has known from an early age that everyone will be satisfied with him as long as he is stupid, despite any expressions to the contrary" (*ibid.*).

The game of "Stupid" is of particular interest in the classroom setting because that atmosphere is also close to ideal for the flowering of its inverse. H. C. Lyon, writing about the kind of life history from which many university faculty members develop, says that "the personality that eventually emerges from all this is typically underlain with a deep sense of inferiority, fear and maladjustment, yet overlain by an almost frantic sense of superiority" (Williams 1958, quoted in Lyon 1971:32). These are harsh words, and certainly the exceptions to them are many, even in the most prestigious and competitive of universities. They may be still less true for those who teach in other settings. Nevertheless, we cannot deny that the role of Teacher has certain built-in attractions for anyone who has serious feelings of inadequacy, and who at the price of attaining tolerable mastery of some limited field of subject matter can thereby be put into a position where he is always right. Entry into this enviable status is particularly easy if the subject matter to be mastered is the language that one acquired automatically as a part of growing up. (I certainly remember this component in my own motivation for becoming a teacher of English as a foreign language.) So, while there are many exceptions, there may be a tendency for the teaching profession to have more than its share of people who are dependent on "the easy victories of the classroom, where they work with people who know less than they do" (Stoke 1969, quoted in Lyon 1971:32).

Under these circumstances, the teacher typically operates in the Parent ego state, with its characteristic furrowed brow, pointing index finger, sighing (mostly outside of class), and its admonition "Now always remember. . ." (Harris 1968:90). The student is treated as a Child: "Students are naturally lazy" (Harris 1968:97), "You never can trust them" (*ibid.*), "The stupids (pun on "students") are late again today." This fits in neatly (the last quotation even fits literally) with the Adapted Child in any student's game of "Stupid," and ensures that whatever learning takes place is "defensive" and "reflective" rather than "receptive" and "productive." (For the meanings of these four terms, see Chapter VII.) A drill provides particularly favorable topography for this erosive confluence of unwholesome ego states, for every line contains its own clearly delineated targets for the teacher's correction and the student's contrition. The symbiosis of the Controlling Parent and the Adapted Child provides a strong defense for this system of classroom psychodynamics, once it has come into being. It seems likely that more language learning is lost through this kind of abuse of drills than through poor design or insufficiently sophisticated technique.

From a psychological point of view, then, drills are often misused.

The obvious question is "Does this mean that teachers (and students) must complete some kind of psychotherapy before they begin their first drill?" Or, "People are people, and personality problems are beyond the scope of the specialist in language." The reply to this sort of objection, I think, is that what may seem unattainable as a destination is still quite feasible as a direction in which to move. We may therefore select our materials and elaborate our techniques with an eye to their potential for making possible Adult-Adult, nonulterior transactions, in which the student's Creative Child—supervised of course by his Adult—feels free to come out and play from time to time. One general suggestion follows on p. 79f. But first, having examined the drilling situation in general, we need to analyze what goes on in that situation.

Drill Procedure

A fairly ordinary procedure for using the typical substitution drill consists of two steps:

1. Teacher reads aloud each line of the drill, and students repeat it. Comprehension is checked. (This step is sometimes unnecessary, and is often omitted.)

2. Teacher reads aloud the first line of drill, plus the cue word for the next line. A student then tries to give the entire next line in response to the cue. The teacher continues through the drill giving successive cues, to which the students reply with the corresponding whole lines.

Although students may repeat step 2 several times, either in class or in the lab, this is ordinarily the last step. When it has been completed up to a certain performance criterion, students go on to the next drill.

It will be worthwhile to look at this common procedure from two points of view: first, in the light of what we know about human memory, and second in the light of the transactional concepts discussed earlier.

With respect to the formation and storage of memories, students in the first of these two steps reproduce the utterances from short-term memory. Research has indicated that oral production of the material carries certain advantages, at least for short-term recall (see Chapter II). If, at the same time, students are conscious of the meaning of what they are saying, then the form and meaning are stored together in a new composite image. Also included in this image are the physical surroundings of classroom or lab, the fact that the image was formed in the context of a manipulative drill, and feelings of empathy, apathy or antipathy toward the instructor. On the other hand, there is unlikely to be found in this newly formed image much that *comes from or leads to* the student's own purposes, needs, or interests.

In the second step, the student is doing cued recall. Although the images that he is recalling were stored only recently, they still must come from what most authorities would call long-term memory (p. 12). They are easier to recall now than they would be five minutes or five hours from now because they have not yet been subjected to much "crowding." Recall is achieved through a combination of rote memory, visual and acoustic images, and *ad hoc* mnemonic devices. As the student recalls the total utterance and finds it to be correct, new relationships among all of these memoranda are perceived, examined and (in the Skinnerian sense) reinforced. This whole experience is then stored in its turn. It is separated by perhaps a minute or two from the corresponding image that was formed during the first step. The two images are distinct, but because they were formed so close together and under virtually identical circumstances, they soon merge as a result of "crowding." The chief value of having in steps 1 and 2 a large number of images containing a given utterance lies less in the number itself than in the opportunity for additional perception, examination and reinforcement of relationships among the parts of the image. One reason for the superiority of distributed over massed practice may be that in the latter, where the same item is repeated several times in succession, the "perceptions" do not have time to change. If this is true, then a student who is required to repeat the same thing many times at increasing speed as a means of "burning the pattern into his brain" (Brown 1968:4) may profit from deliberately shifting the focus of his attention from one part of the utterance to another as the repetitions go on.

So much for the basic drill procedure as seen from the vantage point of research on memory. Let us now look at the same activity in the perspective of Transactional Analysis.

In a drill (as defined on p. 65) control of what is to be said is entirely in the hands of the teacher. The student's performance is therefore necessarily "reflective," and not "productive." He has available to him neither the joys nor the risks of revealing his preferences, his extracurricular activities, or his life history. With regard to communication, he is in the sheltered position of a child, or even of an unborn fetus. It is therefore only natural that his ego state during these two steps of a drill should be that of the Child: the noncreative and therefore the Adapted Child. If that Child happens to be "compliant" (Berne 1964:26) and possessed of a fair amount of language aptitude, it will use the occasion to seek approval from the teacher's Parent by playing a brisk game of "Look-Ma-How-I-Straightened-Up-My-Room" (*i.e.*, by performing very well on the drill). If the teacher's ego state is that of Controlling Parent, he will accept this game as not only natural but desirable; he then will respond with a game of his own, to which we may give the name "That's-My-Kid." If the game is interrupted, the teacher may feel seriously threatened and become noticeably upset.

The perspectives of memory theory and Transactional Analysis are not completely separate from each other. (The first chapter of Harris' book, in fact, draws heavily on the work of one pioneer in memory studies.) The storage of feelings alongside, and inextricably bound together with, linguistic material may cast light on the etiology of a disease that sometimes appears among graduates of even the most advanced language programs. This is lathophobic aphasia (unwillingness to speak for fear of making a mistake). Common symptoms are avoidance of FL situations, addiction to continuous classroom training while resident in a country where the language is spoken, and the feeling that foreigners, some of whom want to practice the student's native language with him, would not also welcome his use of theirs.

A possible contributing cause of this condition, which can produce atrophy of language competence even in the midst of thousands of native speakers, may be that ego states are stored along with basic sentences and structural automaticities. If most or all of these ego states are Adapted Child, then subsequent attempts to speak the language will inexorably revive this ego state along with the words and phrases. Even in so-called "free interaction" sessions, we feel compelled to keep track of and comment on every error. But Rivers (1972:81) tells us that by maintaining an unbending attitude toward mistakes, we may be impeding ourselves from a "great leap forward" (Berne 1964:26; 1972:104).

The suggestion to which I referred on p. 76 is that we add three steps to follow the two that almost everybody uses:

3. Students give sentences from the drill, in any order, without cues. Teacher serves as referee.

From a mnemonic point of view, the students are now doing "immediate and uncued free recall." Some experimental evidence suggests that this activity enhances the ease of future, delayed free recall of the same material (Darley and Murdock 1971). During this step, the student is doing something that only he can do: he is searching through his mind to see which images are available readily, which ones are less clear, and which ones seem to be unusable. This may lead to further perception and examination of relationships. It will at least provide an opportunity for the student to become aware of which elements and relationships he needs to listen for the next time he hears a particular sentence.

With this information about his own inventory of images, a student who is doing free recall may decide to play it safe by selecting only those that are strongest and clearest. Or he may decide to be adventurous, and select an image that he is not sure of, with the hope of filling in the missing parts and so producing a more satisfactory image for use next time. Or, finally, he may choose one that is clear because it is recent, but which he wants to reinforce quickly before it fades. This from the mnemonic point of view.

From the transactional point of view, the student has a range of choices opened to him, among the decisions outlined in the preceding paragraph as well as among the sentences themselves. The availability of choices is the condition that most naturally brings the Adult into play. Moreover, each of the choices is right and acceptable (though he may still make a linguistic mistake); the occasion for reproach, contrition and further reinforcement of the NOT-OK position is absent.

4. Students take turns suggesting sentences which are grammatically similar to those in the drill, but which contain other vocabulary. Teacher again serves as referee.

In this step, as in the preceding one, the student has two kinds of choice open to him: the decision to be bold, cautious, etc., and selection of the lexical items themselves. For the latter, however, he is no longer drawing on material that he has rehearsed within the past few minutes as a part of the drill. The words that he inserts into the pattern may come from very recent learning, or from the very first day of the course. I believe that this is a useful contrast between steps 3 and 4.

On the transactional level, there is a parallel difference between steps 3 and 4: the choices that lie open to the student's Adult now make it possible to express at least some of the things that he (his Parent, his Adult or his Child) would actually like to say. This leads to the final step.

5.   Students use sentences derived from the preceding steps in ways that they hope will draw reactions from teacher or classmates.

One such reaction can be laughter, but others are verbal or nonverbal expressions of interest, sympathy, agreement, disagreement, and so on. The giving of genuine information is yet another possible reaction. At this stage, the whole personality may become engaged with other whole personalities, still within the framework of the drill (Goldstein 1963, quoted in Curran 1968:348).

Although the three extra steps have been discussed separately, in practice they may be merged, and one or another of them may be omitted entirely. Though I have discussed them at length, all of them taken together should consume only 1 to 5 minutes of class time at the end of a drill. I would also like to state explicitly that I am not recommending drills as either the only or the best starter for free communication. It is essential, however, that the teacher have a clear view of the options available, and be aware of what is going on, both mnemonically and in the personality of the student.

Steps 3, 4, and 5 are more than a mere appendage to Steps 1 and 2. They can be much more than just a superficial mitigation of a mechanical and mindless charade (which is how some teachers view drills). The activation of the Adult, which goes along with steps 3 to 5, can extend backward and begin in steps 1 and 2. When this happens, the purpose and also the effects of steps 1 and 2 are transformed. No longer are they simply a relatively sterile means for "practicing and forming habits." Instead, they become a way of exploring a structure, and verifying hypotheses about it. Depending on how they are used, steps 1 and 2 may become an arena for "conscious reasoning" (Diller 1971:73). They may even serve as an additional, very special, medium for meaningful interaction among the people in the classroom.

Exercises

According to the definitions set forth at the beginning of this chapter, a *drill* allows for only one totally acceptable response to each cue item, while an *exercise* allows for more than one. The two types of procedure are alike in that each consists of a series of fairly clearly defined cues and responses to those cues. In this sense, steps 3 to 5 of augmented drill procedure (p. 79f) go beyond the limitations of a drill; because they do not use a steady succession of cues and responses, the direction in which they move is not toward an "exercise" but toward free conversation. On the other hand, if after step 3 the teacher (or a student) had begun to ask questions which would elicit replies that conformed to the pattern of the original drill, then the activity would have been converted into one kind of "exercise."

The remainder of this chapter will be an attempt to examine exercises and some other common classroom events in the same, largely transactional, light in which we have already looked at drills. Obviously, much of what was said about drills applies equally to exercises: they partake of the nature both of "rituals" and of "activities" as Berne uses those terms, and they lend themselves to some of the same "games." Unlike drills, some exercises are also excellent "pastimes."

The exercises that I have in mind are those in which, for example, the teacher asks "What do you see in this room that you like?" and the students respond individually according to their actual feelings. The result is an exercise on affirmative and negative statements, questions and answers in the "simple present" tense. This example and much of what follows are based on a very practical little book by Wilson and Wattenmaker (1973). In this book, a number of other devices are suggested for allowing students to spend a few minutes a day in "sharing honest, personal feelings and experiences." In all of them, honest expression is to be met by respectful listening.

Compare what Berne and Harris have to say about "pastimes." Berne defines a "pastime" as "a series of semi-ritualistic simple, complementary transactions arranged around a single field of material, whose primary object is to structure an interval of time" (Berne 1964:41). An example is "General Motors," generally played by men, in which the first player says, "I like (brand of car) better than (other brand of car) because...," and another replies, "Oh. Well, I'd rather have a (brand of car) than a (brand of car) because..." (46). Berne says that pastimes "have a certain repetitive quality and are in the nature of multiple-choice sentence-completion interchanges"—surely a description of the kind of exercise that we are talking about.

As for their significance, Harris says that pastimes are "a type of social probing where one seeks information about acquaintances in an unthreatening, noncommittal way" (Harris 1968:144). He quotes Berne (1961:98) as saying that "at its best, a pastime is... enjoyed for its own sake and at least it serves as a means of getting acquainted in the hope of achieving the longed-for crasis with another human being. In any case, each participant uses it as an opportunistic way to get whatever primary and secondary gains he can from it" (Harris 1968:144).

A pastime, even in the form of a language exercise, may thus be one stepping-stone toward the kind of intimacy and interpersonal trust which will coax the Natural Child, under Adult supervision, to contribute desirable plasticity and creativeness that we mentioned on p. 68. Learning can then become "receptive" rather than "defensive" (see Chapter VII). But we are also warned that pastimes, like withdrawal, rituals and activities, can keep people apart (Harris 1968:146). The crucial factor may be the *kind of response* that the student gets when he does express his own opinions, preferences or feelings.

From a transactional point of view, the easiest response for the teacher to give is also the worst. If the teacher is primarily aware of his own need for fresh linguistic fillers to illustrate his precious pattern, he will greedily gobble up the student's offerings, run them through the machine, and forget about them. This response provides the student with only a minimum of "stroking" (recognition that he is present).

A less obvious but more encouraging type of response is central to a course in "Liberated Spanish" which Keith Sauer has conducted in Fresno. The most interesting feature of this course is that from the very beginning, students are taught words and structures that will enable them to *disagree* with one another. [If I say something, I get more than a perfunctory recognition that *someone* has said *something;* from a fellow student or from the teacher, I get recognition of *what* I have said, and if the rejoinder is addressed to me, I also get recognition that *I* was the one who said it.] This is much more powerful stroking; even being disagreed with is better than being ignored (Berne 1964:15). Psychodynamically, Sauer's idea is very sound. It is a more powerful counterpart of step 5 in the drill procedure and makes a very worthwhile addition to the standard procedure for this particular type of exercise.

More generally, exercises of this kind are potentially fertile ground for producing what people live by; that this ground is so often barren is both unnecessary and unfortunate. What keeps people alive, according to Berne—what "keeps their spinal cords from shriveling up"—is "stroking," which means being recognized and responded to by other human beings. This is the basis of the need for "acceptance." In Berne's sense, to say that one person "accepts" another is not to say that he approves of him or likes him; it is only to say that he is willing to spend more time with him (1971:9), and this implies continued "stroking" of one kind or another. To feel "accepted" is therefore to feel that someone else is willing to continue noticing me and responding to me. This is Maslow's "need for belonging," which is prior to his "need for esteem" and approval (Maslow 1970:43-45).

The usual teacher-response to the student in this type of exercise is addressed almost exclusively to the narrow "linguistic-correctness" sector of the student's esteem need, and only minimally to his need for belonging.

Curran, in his unconventional system for adult learning of foreign languages (Chapter 8), makes much of the need for the knower to respond to the learner in a manner that conveys "warmth, acceptance and understanding." He further emphasizes that this sort of reaction on the part of the knower may help the learner to regress to a more open, Child-like state. What is particularly of interest to readers of this chapter is his application of this principle in the field of adult language learning (Curran 1961, 1966, 1968, 1972; Laforge 1971 and 1975; Bégin 1971).

If the feeling of having been heard and understood has such a powerful therapeutic effect, then there may be a place for it in the context of an exercise. For example, the practice of making one student responsible for remembering what another student said, and reporting it on request, may be a wholesome one. Thus, Student A must notice that the thing in the classroom that B likes to look at is the clock, and that his reason for liking to look at it is that it is always moving. B, in turn, must remember that C likes to look at his desk top because of the interesting carvings on it. They must be ready to recall this information and give it at the end of the exercise, or even at later sessions of the class.

Summary

This chapter has treated a very few classroom activities largely within a single theoretical framework. It has included a few concrete suggestions for modifying or augmenting techniques in ways that are consistent with this framework. The reader who sees only what is in this chapter will have missed the point of it. The concepts of Transactional Analysis are not the only ones that could be used in exploring the "meaning" of these kinds of drill and exercise activity. More important, what has been said about these activities could be said, *mutatis mutandis*, about dialog memorization or the use of short anecdotes or the exploitation of 35mm slides; the concrete suggestions are given primarily to clarify the principles from which they have been derived, and are not intended as methodological prescriptions. At the same time, Chapters IV and V together provide the basis for a general view of method, which stands at the beginning of Part 3.

VI
Between Teacher and Student: The Language Class as a Small Group

In Chapters IV and V, we looked at some of the things that go on inside the student as he encounters various aspects of the process of language study. In this chapter, we shall begin by taking a hasty glance at the teacher, and go on to summarize a bit of the literature on power structures, trust, and "community."

The Teacher

The concentration in Chapters IV and V on the anxieties, frustrations, and defensive actions of the student may have left the impression that the teacher is relatively free from such feelings, or has no need to engage in such maneuvers. This, of course, is not the case. Teachers are human too!

For reasons that one may darkly suspect, the literature about what goes on inside the teacher is much slimmer than the literature about students. The language teaching profession seems particularly to have been neglected: Silberman's well known *Crisis in the Classroom* (1970) contains no significant reference to our field; Miles (1964:473) mentions foreign language learning as one area in which we need to use "an analysis of here-and-now events," but he does not elaborate; Lyon's book (1971) on humanistic education contains specific examples from mathematics, science, and native-language teaching, but none from foreign languages. Yet the fears and anxieties of teachers are probably no less than those of their students; they differ only in form. Teachers, too, are human!

As the terms are used in this chapter, *fear* differs from *anxiety* partly in that "fear" is occasioned by external, relatively objective threats: an onrushing car, a sinister-looking group in the shadows near the bus-stop, seeing one's child pick and swallow what may have been a poisonous mushroom. On the other hand, a large component of "anxiety" comes from inner or subjective conditions (Jersild 1955:27).

The inner, subjective conditions that contribute to anxiety are, to a large extent, the same "NOT-OK" feelings that we talked about in Chapter V. A person in the occupational status "teacher" may seek protection or relief from those feelings by operating in the Parent state. The teacher patterns his Parent stage after one or more of those powerful figures who in his own early childhood were the very embodiment of OK-ness, goodness and adequacy. From raw materials such as these, he may construct an image of himself which he shows to the public, and in which he also comes to believe.

Rogers (in Hayakawa 1962:229) describes the self-concept as "an organized configuration of perceptions of the self which are admissible to awareness." If, as Darwin said, self-preservation is the first law of life, then preservation of the symbolic self may be the fundamental principle of human motivation (Hayakawa 1962:226). Threats to this image therefore constitute a rich and inexhaustible source of anxieties. Disparities between those motives which are admissible to awareness, and those that are not, are the basis for a wide variety of "games."

This is not to say that everything teachers do is merely an expression of one or more anxieties, or that all their actions are moves in unwholesome games. Mutually respectful, nonexploitative relationships *can* exist in a language class, and sometimes do. Even some "games" make social contributions which outweigh the complexity of their motivations (Berne 1964:163). The results of unacknowledged motives still may be benign.

Thus Curran (1972:114) speaks of the creative thinker as being "sick to teach"—as having a powerful and partly irrational craving to have people understand him on the intellectual level. This is in addition to his basic human need for acceptance on the emotional plane. Any teacher who plans a lesson with care and imagination is, in that respect, a creative thinker with a "sickness" to receive appreciation. A native-speaking teacher (or even a nonnative one who has made a heavy personal investment in the target culture) may see learning of the language as acceptance of him and his culture, and failure to learn as rejection. This is another normal and generally benign kind of "sickness," to which language teachers are more susceptible than most of their colleagues. The passion to help one's students grow in their own individuality, becoming emotionally more whole and intellectually more self-sufficient (Lyon 1971:197), is perhaps the most benign of teacher attitudes. It requires great personal strength. (What are its sources?)

"A teacher cannot make much headway in understanding others or in helping others to understand themselves unless he is endeavoring to understand himself. If he is not engaged in this endeavor, he will continue to see those whom he teaches through the bias and distortions of his own unrecognized needs, fears, desires, anxieties, and hostile impulses" (Jersild 1955:14). In the pages which follow, therefore, we shall look at some of the ways in which a single act may be compatible with one purpose on the public, acknowledgeable, social level, and with a quite unrelated, not-so-acknowledgeable motive on the psychological level. In other words, we shall explore a few of the "games" that language teachers sometimes play. This material is set out in the shape of seven replies to a questionnaire. The responses are imaginary, but they are drawn from observation of numerous very real teachers, chief among whom is the author. Although they make rather speculative use of transactional terminology, they are not intended as a poor man's guide to individual psychoanalysis. They are only an attempt to suggest some of the complexities of teacher motivation (Items *b* and *c*), and to show how challenges (Item *d*) to the self-concept (Item *a*) may contribute to anxiety.

The four items of the questionnaire are the following. (Note that while Items *c* and *d* in each reply are potentially consistent with Item *b* in the same reply, they do not necessarily go along with it.)

QUESTIONNAIRE

I am a teacher, and as a teacher _____ (*a*) _____
This is true or necessary because _____ (*b*) _____
   (Social level: real reason, or publicly acceptable excuse?)
I also feel this way because _____ (*c*) _____
   (Psychological level: additional bonus, or actual motive?)
What bothers me most is _____ (*d*) _____

*****

The seven sets of replies are given below:

1. *a.* I know my subject matter.
   b. I am the students' link with the realities of the foreign language.
   c. Whatever I do must be accepted as right.
   (A Parent posture, but related to a NOT-OK Child who is trying to escape being "wrong.")
   d. Someone claiming that I have made a mistake.
2. *a.* I know more than my students know.
   b. I am a native speaker of the language, or have studied it for many years.
   c. I can always win the basic Child-Child game of "Mine is Better."
   d. A student who has gotten into my class in spite of coming from a home where the language is used, or having lived where it is spoken.
3. *a.* I must correct my students when they make mistakes.
   b. I am their link with the realities of the foreign language.
   c. In correcting them (or in praising them when they are right), I identify with my own OK-Parent sources, who were always evaluating my conduct for me, who was a NOT-OK Child.
   d. The suggestion that I could teach as well or better if I would limit my interventions so as to require and allow more independent mental activity from the student.
4. *a.* I must decide what is to happen in the class, and when.
   b. I have had more experience in language classes than the students have had, as well as training in linguistics and pedagogy.
   c. In controlling my students, I identify with my own OK-Parent sources (perhaps my actual parents, or my own teachers, or some combination of these), who were always controlling me, a NOT-OK

Child. Besides, it's a matter of respect, which I as a NOT-OK Child never got.

   d. Petitions, suggestions or complaints from students regarding my procedures.

5. *a.* I should do my best to meet the expressed needs of my students.

   b. Their expressions of desire or preference can provide me with valuable hints about what they are ready to respond to.

   c. By complying with their requests, I may be able to win from them the kind of OK strokes that my Child has always lacked. Or perhaps by doing so I may identify with my own Parent sources as a provider of necessities and a granter of boons.

   d. Close, authoritarian supervision, or a heavy workload, or whatever prevents me from complying with my students' requests.

6. *a.* I respond to opportunities as they arise; I therefore need not prepare for classes.

   b. Fresh material is generally more stimulating than material that is cut-and-dried.

   c. My Child doesn't like to carry responsibility and, anyhow, it would rather spend the time in other ways.

   d. Suggestions that I would teach better if I made detailed, written lesson plans. To do so would restrict my creativity, cramp my style.

7. *a.* I should tend to business.

   b. If too much time is spent in ways that are unrelated to the task at hand, the task will not get completed.

   c. By limiting the scope of my contacts with the students, I can avoid expressing or perceiving emotion, thus keeping from view the Child that I either distrust or am ashamed of.

   d. Suggestions that I should encourage the expression of honest feelings as a part of the learning experience.

*****

Notice that if we paste together the *b* items from the seven replies shown in the questionnaire we come out with the qualifications of a rather fine teacher:

Someone who knows the language either natively or very well, with thorough knowledge of the subject matter. Has been trained in linguistics and pedagogy, and has also had classroom experience.

Tends to business, but uses fresh material and is open to suggestions from students.

If in the same way we combine all the c items, we arrive at a picture of a miserable wretch who is compulsively passing on to his students the same unpleasantness that he experienced at the hands of his own elders. This is a person who will resist bitterly any attempt to deprive him of "the gratifications that reside in the central, highly-differentiated teacher role" and who has strong "fears of fallibility and loss of status" (Miles 1964:470). This is also the person about whom Lyon wrote the words that we quoted in Chapter V (p. 75), and who leads Williams to assert that professors are more likely than most people to ridicule ignorance, to beat down imagination and creativeness, and to be unsympathetic toward universal human weaknesses (in Lyon 1971).

It should be emphasized that the picture which we have painted on the social level (Items b) and the picture on the psychological level (Items c) are not necessarily found together: they may be found in the same person, but either can, of course, exist separate from the other. Most of us probably represent some kind of mixture, for a conscious wish (Items a, for example) usually has more than one motivation (Maslow 1970:22) and drives are interrelated, not mutually exclusive (Maslow 1970:25).

To say that our laudable aims (Items a) sometimes rest on motivations that we would rather not talk about is not a condemnation either of the aims themselves or of the motivations. It is merely analogous to the observation that a person may produce a linguistic analysis (or write a book like this one) as a part of a game of "Mine Is Better" or "Look-Ma-No-Hands." The analysis may be valid or invalid, and the thesis of this book worthy or unworthy of attention, independent of the psychological state of the people who wrote them. But there is one respect in which the analogy between teacher and writer fails. Insofar as a teacher is working from c-type motives, he is susceptible to threats of the kinds represented by Items d. These threats produce anxieties, which in turn become the occasion for defensive reactions on the part of the teacher. These reactions become an involuntary, partially subliminal, but for all that more compelling, component of the teacher's input to the continuing interchange between him and the students. Jersild, a veteran observer of the educational scene, believes that "many teachers and students have lived with anxiety day after day, scarcely knowing that the burden might be lightened . . . Schools and colleges have usually offered them little in the way of help except academic activities that sidestep anxiety, or perhaps even increase it" (Jersild 1955:8). He further points out that "there are few unforbidden, frank and direct channels for expressing hostility in education but ["and therefore"?! EWS] much of what is done in the name of education or scholarship is, indirectly, a means of venting hostility" (9). I wonder to what extent this statement is also true for "love" or "affection," as well as for "hostility."

What, then, is the teacher to do in the face of his internal inconsistencies and the complexities of his own personality? Clearly, he must get himself sorted out, and that is a job for the Adult (p. 68f). But how is the Adult to get into control? Jakobovits and Gordon (1974) do not use the terminology of Eric Berne, but one of the recurring themes of their book is exactly that. Their chief suggestion is that the teacher participate in "Encounter Transaction Workshops." On a more immediate and mechanical level, I suspect that one of the most important effects of Interaction Analysis (Moskowitz 1968, 1971, 1974; Krumm 1973) is to put the teacher into his Adult.

This ends our very brief look "inside the teacher." In Chapters IV and V, we examined in greater detail some of the things that go on inside the learner. We turn now to the interactions that go on between teachers and learners.

Authority Structures

The most fundamental fact about any social system, including a language class, is the way the *power* issues have been settled (Ilfeld and Lindeman 1971:588; Gibb 1964:283; Bennis 1964:251). On the chessboard of academic-style education, the most *powerful* single piece is the teacher. Society invests him with authority, which is the right to exercise *power*. The personal style with which he wields that authority is a principal determinant of the *power* structure of the class. It is at these issues that we shall look first.

Zaleznik and Moment see four prototype patterns of authority. The first of these they call *paternal-assertive*. This pattern is characterized by aggressiveness, dominance, and initiation of interaction on the part of the authority figure. This figure avoids tender feelings, but may be deeply concerned with the advancement and reward of subordinates, particularly the ones who accept his or her form of authority (1964:273). One of the problems common under this type of authority structure is that the subordinates—in our case, the language learners—may develop anxiety about their own capacity to act assertively (274).

Zaleznik and Moment's second authority pattern is *maternal-expressive*. Here, the leader avoids initiation and aggressiveness, but concentrates instead on creating affective ties with subordinates, exercising control over them by withdrawing affection and thereby threatening them with rejection. If the subordinates fail to get enough attention from this kind of authority figure, they may react with anger or with depression (273f).

In the *fraternal-permissive* prototype, the leader consciously minimizes any status differentiation, aiming instead at equality. Authority resides in something outside the group, such as a task (learning a language, for example, or preparing for work in a foreign country) or a set of ideals (various "integrative" motivations). The needs of the subordinates appear to dominate in this relationship. The leader shares with his subordinates as much responsibility as possible, and tries to encourage them (273).

In many ways, this third pattern might seem to be the one at which a personally secure language teacher ought to aim. Considerable evidence indicates that when subordinates exercise significant amounts of control over what is going on, their performance and productivity improve (Bachman 1964:272). Much is being written these days in our own field about individualization of foreign language instruction, and "student-centered" education is again becoming stylish. Zaleznik and Moment, however, warn that the fraternal style may not be ideal for a task-oriented group, and a language class is, by definition, task-oriented at least to a large extent. The emphasis on the group itself, with corresponding de-emphasis of evaluation and status differentiation, may keep the needed work from getting done (274); if this happens, it, in turn, may produce anxieties that are related to the professional or academic reasons which caused the students to take the course in the first place. In the terminology of Lambert, if the "integrative" side of the class crowds out the "instrumental," there is likely to be trouble. But even without this kind of concern, there are some students who simply need a given style of authority of one parental variety or the other (Carl Rogers in LaForge 1971:58).

One may speculate that the supreme affront to a "paternal" leader is refusal to obey; that the most upsetting experience for a "maternal" leader is to feel that he or she has not been properly appreciated; and that the ultimate disappointment for a leader who has aimed at a "fraternal" style is to realize that others will not give up their demand that he be parental (LaForge 1971:48).

The fourth and last authority pattern that Zaleznik and Moment list is the *rational-procedural.* It avoids some of the pitfalls of the other three by minimizing emotion and interpersonal relationships. The person in charge seeks to invoke the constraints of impersonal authority, in the form of objectives, laws and regulations—or an externally imposed syllabus or a very detailed set of teaching materials (273). Unfortunately, however, this prototype also has its disadvantage: by failing to reach individuals at sufficiently deep levels in their emotional experience, it may produce very little involvement or creativity (274).

If authority systems in language teaching were arranged along a continuum from authoritarian to permissive, the first extreme would surely find its embodiment in the work of Borden and Busse (1925), "speech correctionists" of the 1920s. The people with whom they worked were not called "students," but "patients," many of whom suffered from "defects of foreign dialect." These defects were apparently regarded as being comparable to catarrh or a cleft palate. The style of "treatment" employed by these authors to remove one common symptom was the following (183):

> If the patient stubbornly persists in substituting T as in TOWN for TH as in THIN . . . hold the blade of his tongue forcibly down in its proper position by means of a wire form (called) a "fricator." If he persists in substituting TH for S, push his tongue back into its proper position with a forked metal brace . . . known technically as a "fraenum fork."

The therapist is warned that once the patient can make the sound in isolation, he must practice it in larger units. He must also "ruthlessly eliminate the old defective sound from his speech—even from colloquial speech with intimate friends" (188). The fraenum fork and fricator make Borden and Busse's method seem bizarre to us, but how many present-day methods are more sophisticated in their approach to personality, or less authoritarian in their assumptions about the distribution of power?

Zaleznik and Moment find that there is much evidence that, under certain conditions, a participative and relatively permissive style of leadership has been accompanied by marked improvement in group productivity, morale, and emotional involvement (432). The reasons why this is so are not entirely clear, but these authors suggest that a major factor is that in this pattern there is more attention to what they call "reality-testing." But if "reality-testing" is, in fact, the essential element, they point out, it is compatible with a great range of leadership styles, from permissive to stern (*ibid.*).

Curran apparently thought along the same lines when he wrote about "the maturity and therapy of limits" (1968: Chapter 10). In a language classroom, we tend to think first about the limits imposed by the subject matter, beginning with the structure and vocabulary of the language itself. The student certainly needs to learn to deal with these. But in a class, as in any group process, the very presence of others imposes limits on each student (1968:211). There are also, of course, the limits that any human being carries from his physical nature and his past history. The struggle, at once collective and individual, to live with these limits is an essential element of the process of maturing (1968:213). It is also a principal source of the latent or active forces which exist in every classroom, potentially supportive of learning, but seldom harnessed to the constructive purposes of the teacher (Bradford 1960, quoted in LaForge 1971:47; Miles 1964:469).

As students set out to test reality in its many aspects, they meet the teacher at every turn. There are at least four ways in which this is true. Most obviously, perhaps, the teacher's culturally conferred status makes him a link with the reality of those rewards and punishments (grades, promotions, recommendations) that society attaches to performance in the course. From another point of view, his superior knowledge of the language and its related subject matter make him an indispensable link with the realities of whatever content the students hope to learn. Third, the teacher's training and accumulated experience mean that he is a potentially useful medium through whom to deal with the realities of organizing the work to be done. Finally, because of his pivotal position in the classroom, the teacher is, for each individual, one important link with the realities that are represented by the other students.

In each of these respects, the teacher is a door that is either open or closed. Or, to change the figure of speech, the teacher is a bridge. Before a student is willing to venture out on a reality-testing expedition in one or another of these directions, he checks to see whether the bridge that leads in that direction looks safe. If it appears shaky or slippery he will, according to his temperament, be cautious or aggressive, obsequious or resentful, but learning will be affected (Jersild 1955:62; Curran 1968:231). This brings us to the crucially important question of building mutual trust in a small group such as a language class.

Interpersonal Trust

There is a fairly large body of literature on this subject. Perhaps its most fundamental and, at the same time, most controversial concept is that trust is produced by behavior that can be changed, and that, in turn, it is functionally related to desirable changes in the behavior of groups (Giffin 1967:233). In contrast to this idea is the view, held by many teachers, that "people are the way they are": a teacher who presumes to try to do anything with adolescent or adult students except impart information to them is aiming at a goal that is as inappropriate as it is impossible. If students are assumed to be "plastic learners in a fixed cultural environment" (Benne 1964:24; Miller 1964), these teachers seem to regard them as plastic only in the most narrowly cognitive sense, and as being in other respects quite rigid.

The primal importance of trust is implied in Gibb's summary of the deepest and earliest concerns in the life of a group. They occur, he says, in the following order: first "acceptance," then "data flow," then "goal formation," and finally "control" (Gibb 1964:283). In everyday English, this means that people must feel relatively secure with those around them before they will say what is really on their minds; that only after a group knows what its members have on their minds can it figure out what it wants to do; and that there is no point in trying to decide how to use the time, energy and other resources of a group until its goals have become clear.

Gibb was writing primarily about "T-Groups," which have no pre-established goals or control mechanisms. In a language class, of course, (the intellectual parts of) the goals are already well defined and (the administrative aspects of) the control mechanism fairly clear. I believe, however, that if we take into account the nonintellectual and nonadministrative aspects, Gibb's scenario is valid in our world as well as in his. Koch, in fact, found a very similar sequence in intercultural workshops in Germany: the workshop atmosphere reduced inhibitions and established an initial level of trust; within this atmosphere, participants felt a strong need to communicate with one another ("data flow"); and in this context, superior language learning took place (1972). Levertov, teaching creative writing to native speakers, observed that her students seldom made really sincere suggestions as long as they felt that they were among strangers whom they could not trust (1970:159).

A brief article by Giffin summarized much of what had been written up to 1967 concerning the variables which tend to build trust or destroy it. Some of the factors which Giffin lists are the following:

1. B is more likely to trust A if B feels that A has acted in a way which has shown conditional trust in B; and if A seems to expect that B will in turn act in a trustworthy way; and if A indicates that he himself is ready to reciprocate whatever trust B shows for him.

2. B is more likely to trust A if A makes an enforceable promise to him.

3. Certain kinds of communication from A tend to increase B's trust in him:
    a. Communication in which B feels that A is describing what he sees, rather than passing judgment on it.
    b. Communication in which B feels that A is interested in solving a problem, rather than in controlling him or someone else.
    c. Communication in which A seems to be stating tentative rather than final conclusions.
    d. Communication which B sees as spontaneous and sincere, not motivated by some concealed purpose.
    e. Communication which means to B that A is personally involved in the exchange, and not just an aloof observer.

To anyone who has read Chapter V, these five criteria for communication will have a familiar ring. Points 3a-c mean, in transactional terminology, that a trustworthy communicator is a person who is operating in his Adult (p. 68f); points 3d-e say that the communicator who wants to be trusted must avoid the appearance of engaging in ulterior transactions (p. 69).

These same five criteria are also reminiscent of some of the characteristics of what Curran calls a "counseling response": warmth, understanding, and acceptance, the communicator involved but at the same time able to deal objectively with emotional data (1961:81). As students explore the realities of the limits we have listed above, they often become anxious. They may then react against the person or persons who are the voice or the occasion of these limits. Here we have described in three different ways the kind of response by teacher or parent which can aid such a student to begin to distinguish the limits from the people who represent them, and so to deal with his own negative reactions and conflicts (Curran 1968:215). This is a major step in building an atmosphere of mutual trust.

In this light, we may take a fresh look at what is essential in the role of "teacher." As Chastain has rightly pointed out (1971:370), the teacher should first of all appear to the students as a strong person, a source of stability. Otherwise their deepest need, at the level of security, will remain unfulfilled. Attempts to motivate them at less fundamental levels will then prove largely futile. This does not mean, however, that strength can be manifested only by ubiquity, omnipotence, omniscience, or inflexibility. Frank (1964:449), writing not about teachers but about trainers in T-groups, said that dependency on the trainer should be limited to looking to him for (general) guidance on how to proceed, and for clarification of what is happening.

A language class is not a T-group, of course. The most inevitable difference is that the former is committed to the task of learning a language, while the latter has no outside commitments at all. We must therefore assign to the teacher the additional role of an information source. But some of the activities at which teachers spend great amounts of time do not fall clearly under any of these three rubrics. None of these functions, for example, requires the teacher to emit a steady stream of praise and blame, or of confirmation and correction. None requires him to be one of the participants in every exchange, or to do 50% or more of the talking, or to give the students detailed guidance at every step. None requires him to display either wittiness or erudition, or to be "buddies" with his students. While any of these may be compatible with good teaching, none is essential. Each of them, furthermore, is sometimes used by teachers for their own personal reasons; when this happens, these kinds of behavior may begin to interfere with learning.

A Goal: "Voice in Community"

The preceding parts of this chapter have perhaps concentrated too much on the seamy side of teacher-student relationships. We turn now to the more positive side, and to description of a desirable style of dynamics for the language classroom. We shall label it "Voice in Community."

Rivers (1968:167) says that a class "consists of individuals who have gradually been welded into a group with some knowledge of each other's activities, and some interest in each other's affairs." This description implies that a certain amount of "data flow" is taking place within such a class and, in turn, this means that some level of interpersonal trust exists. It does not, however, tell us how pervasive is the trust, or the "depth" from which the "data" are flowing.

One of the few sustained examinations of the role of group forces in language learning is found in the Northeast Conference report on "motivation" (Tursi 1970). Libit and Kent, in their contribution to that report, mention the obvious fact that "accomplishment is a source of motivation" (57). This observation relates principally to the level of "esteem" in the student's "hierarchy of needs." They precede that statement, however, with the more profound observation that "fear is one of the first obstacles to be eliminated" (55). This, of course, is the deeper "security" need in the same hierarchy. They go on to urge teachers to remember that "it is a 'soul'—a self—that the student wants to express in the foreign language" (58). Curran goes even further when he says that a student learning a language under conditions of minimum anxiety may actually develop a "new language self" (1961:92). He would concur with Libit and Kent in emphasizing the importance of the group as a source of motivation in foreign language learning (Tursi 1970:79), and in their belief that "a classroom *can* be an intimate place where each student knows his place in the group, and knows that others recognize him" (80) (emphasis added). Libit and Kent, Curran (1972), Wilson and Wattenmaker (1973), and Rivers (1972) are unusually rich sources of concrete ideas for expediting "data flow" in language class.

Lambert, too, agrees that "the challenge for the teacher is to go beyond the mere achievement motives of students, and to link language teaching with more appropriate and more productive motives" (Tursi 1970:87). Some of these motives, surely, must be found in the many "informal and quasi-formal communities" that may come into being either in the classroom or outside it (Nelson 1970:61). In such a community all members—"teacher" as well as "students"—see that if any one of them is to get ahead, he must depend on the others. People who perceive themselves to be in such a relationship tend to act in ways that are consistent with that perception (Loomis 1959:305). Then, as realities come to be not only experienced individually but also shared, learning becomes more profound for students and teacher alike (Levertov 1970:188).

Some of the most perceptive remarks about classroom communities appear in a brief essay by George Elliott (1970:50), a teacher of creative writing. They are worth quoting at some length:

> A good class pulls together into a kind of community. It is only an occasional community (and) there is no way to prescribe how to bring such a community into being . . . Freedom to make or not to make a community of a class is essential if you are to make it at all.

> An alternative to squatting sequestered in the fastness of pedantry is to strive in the classroom to let come into being a fragile community. The extraordinary ingredient in making communities is not possessing the power to make them, but exercising that power, wanting them enough to risk failure. Our life is so far from nature now . . . that many no longer know they have the power of communion, of making even fragile communities, and many have too little hope of exercising that power successfully even to try, even to want to try. The faith must be restored. What can we who are believers but not great prophets do to restore this faith except exercise that power as best we can?

It is in a community such as this that the student can, in several senses, find his "voice." Most literally, he is more likely to use his larynx for purposes other than mimicry. In addition, and more important, his unique presence will be felt by those around him, and his personality will express itself in what he says (Hawkes 1970:96). If the teacher's own ideas about how he ought to act are not too rigid, he too may come to have a voice in this kind of community (Gibb 1964:302). If he is fortunate, he will even find himself sharing with other human beings his knowledge, experience and enthusiasm on subjects of mutual interest!

Part 3. Method

VII
A General View
of Method

In Part 1 we looked at some of the research that has been done on memory. The most important single concept that emerged was "depth." In Part 2 we explored this dimension as it applies to the foreign language classroom, using insights drawn from Abraham Maslow, Eric Berne, T.A. Harris and others. In Part 3 we shall examine what all of this may mean for the design and implementation of methods in our field. In doing so, we shall not attempt to set up yet another method to compete with those already in existence. Instead, we shall aim in this chapter for statements that will respond to those elements of soundness and truth which are to be found in any method that has survived long enough to have received a name. In Chapters VIII, IX and X, we shall apply the principles of the present chapter to discussions of a number of quite different methods, all of which are considered, in some circles at least, as extremely dubious.

AN AUTOBIOGRAPHICAL STATEMENT

A number of recent writers on methodology have seemed to believe that, as far as language teaching is concerned, the two boundary posts of the inhabited world are "audiolingual habit theory" and "cognitive code-learning theory," and that any teacher or textbook finds a place somewhere between these extremes (Chastain 1971:5f and 154f; Hok 1972:263; Mueller 1971; Ney 1974; Oskarsson 1973:251). If this is true, then I myself was born, professionally, in Audiolinguia and have spent most of my career there. A few years ago, however, being attracted by the more fertile fields of Cognitia, I emigrated and took up residence in the new land (though I still retain many good friends in the old country), hoping that after fulfilling the requirements I might be granted citizenship there. Before that could happen, however, something caused me to change my mind and leave Cognitia, not to return to Audiolinguia but to explore Terra Incognita—the unknown land beyond (or beneath?) the boundary posts. I found that, although I was not the first language teacher to set foot on this terrain, the things that I was seeing were almost completely omitted from the literature of our profession. I discovered that to say that audiolingualism and cognitive code learning are the polar extremes in language teaching is a bit like saying that the poles of ancient thought were Rome and Byzantium, or that all significant political activity today takes place on a continuum bounded by Washington and Moscow. To say so would be inaccurate; worse, it would be antiheuristic: it would make us less likely to discover for ourselves what else there is in this world.

THE RIDDLE

One of the circumstances that turned my eyes toward Terra Incognita may be stated in the form of a riddle:

> In the field of language teaching, Method A is the logical contradiction of Method B: if the assumptions from which A claims to be derived are correct, then B cannot work, and vice versa. Yet one colleague is getting excellent results with A and another is getting comparable results with B. How is this possible?

This riddle has troubled me for a quarter-century—ever since I discovered that the first method I learned to use was not the only good way to teach. Sometimes the same riddle (and I believe that it *is* ultimately the same riddle) takes a different form:

Why does Method A (or B) sometimes work so beautifully and at other times so poorly?

Method, in Anthony's sense (1963), differs from method concerning the place of memorization, or the role of visual aids, or the importance of controlling and sequencing structure and vocabulary, or how the teacher should respond when a student makes a mistake, or the number of times a student should hear a correct model, or whether to give the explanation before or after practice or not at all, and so forth.

To try to reconcile all the answers that we get to questions like these leads to chaos if we remain on the plane on which these matters usually are discussed. I believe, however, that if we leave that plane, which is defined by linguistic analysis and overt classroom behavior, we may find that each method, when used well, fulfills in its own way a set of requirements which go beneath and beyond any one of them. The answer to just what these requirements are lies largely in Terra Incognita. This chapter is therefore a letter from a traveler, rather than an authoritative road map. More than the other chapters in this book, it is written in the first person singular because it describes the view through the eyes of one man.

AN OBITER DICTUM ON RESEARCH

The usual modern answer to unresolved questions such as those listed above is to recommend that there be more research, and that teachers try to stay abreast of it. The call to "keep up with the (*i.e.*, our) latest research" (*passim*) is based on a belief that past failures have been due to insufficient *knowledge*, and that therefore what we need is to know more. If, on the other hand, we start from the assumption that past failures—and successes—have come from the degree of *wisdom* with which we have handled what we have known at the time, then the urgency of research appears smaller. From this same position, the persons of the teacher and of the teacher-trainer—the very factors that much "controlled research" and much "materials development" seek to eliminate or to become independent of—begin to loom large. But such a conclusion is repugnant to us as creatures of a culture that has so committed us to exactness, interchange-ability, predictability, and economies of scale. So we flee back to the temples of science, to its priesthood that can feed us on reliability and validity, no matter in how small morsels, and whose "pie in the sky" will become available for eating after all "further needed research" has been completed, replicated, field-tested and applied. (For a similar view, see Jakobovits and Gordon 1974:93ff.)

I personally feel toward research very much as I feel toward motherhood: I am in favor of it, I respect it, I hate to think where we would all be without a certain amount of it; but I am biologically unequipped to perform it.

This is not to say that from a psychodynamic point of view research is to be scoffed at. But its worth now becomes heuristic rather than prescriptive: instead of expecting research findings to tell us how we ought to design and conduct our courses, we look to them for light which may *or may not* help us to perceive more readily what is going on in a total, particular human experience "as it really is" (Curran 1972:67). In Curran's terms, research may thus be an aid toward "incarnation." In transactional terms, it ceases to be a (sometimes fickle, always oracular*) Controlling Parent figure. Instead, it becomes "a vast store of data . . . (which may be) a burden or a boon depending on how appropriate it is to (a given situation), and on whether or not it has been updated by the (practition-er's) Adult" (Harris 1968:46).

Four words, useful in sketching what the title of this chapter calls "a general view of method," are the terms of two polar distinctions. Perhaps the easiest way to describe those distinctions is to begin with an incident that I observed recently: A Turkish class in its 30th hour of instruction was drilling itself on a pattern that usually is reserved for about the 150th hour. With very few interventions by the teacher, the students were making up the drill as they went along, proceeding with deliberation, but smoothly. There was noticeable lack of tension. As their supervisor, I complimented them and their teacher, at which one of them replied in Turkish "we-thank-you," a form that he had never heard. This happened to be the very form that had been the subject of discussion among the

---

*This word is used here in the sense of "resembling an oracle in some way, as in solemnity, wisdom, authority, obscurity, ambiguity, dogmatism." (*Webster's Second International Dictionary*)

staff only a few days earlier. We had noted that even our advanced students failed to come up with this form when they needed it, preferring instead to use *teşekkür ederim* "I-thank-you" as an all-purpose translation of English "thank you." So this particular class session was doubly delightful to me. How did it happen?

I'm not sure, of course. But the following are my best guesses.

PERFORMANCE: PRODUCTIVE OR REFLECTIVE

First of all, we need to distinguish between two kinds of *performance:* that which is *productive* and that which is *reflective,* or echoic. Insofar as a student is bouncing back what the teacher is throwing at him, his performance is reflective. The extreme case is mimicry of pronunciation, where the meaning of a word, even if the student knows it, is unimportant. But substitution drills, transformation drills, and other conventional kinds of grammatical calisthenics are almost as completely reflective as phonetic mimicry is. Even retelling of stories, answering questions about a dialog, or discussing a reading selection, though they contain some elements of productivity, are still largely reflective.

Insofar as performance is productive, on the other hand, the student does not start from the assigned task of following a language model that the teacher or textbook has provided. Instead, he starts with something that he wants to say and with a person to whom he wants to say it. He then draws on the models that are available within himself, in order to fulfill his purpose. The Turkish class that I described above had been working productively, rather than reflectively, for most of its 30 hours. The students had been both allowed and required to notice what they were doing, and to piece together their own individual pictures of how Turkish works. This is, I suspect, the reason why one of them arrived quite naturally and spontaneously at the form "we-thank-you." It also may account for the performance on which I had complimented them in the first place.

Reflectivity and Productivity in the Literature

Language teachers have produced a constant flow of articles about how to get back from students the responses that we want them to give; we like to worry about the best way to design materials for this purpose, and the most appropriate kinds of teacher behavior; we construct fascinating and sometimes useful models of what must go on in the student's head as he acquires the ability to repeat a dialog or go nimbly through a drill. Whenever we do these things, we are concentrating on *reflectivity*, and it is this variety of performance that has received almost all our attention. From this point of view we ask ourselves "how?"—"how" do learners use their brains in learning (Wardhaugh 1971:19), or "how" does the learner become able to encode or decode grammatical sequences? (Titone 1970:47); and we analyze the various levels of the linguistic side of "what" they say (Jakobovits 1970:19f); but we do not ask "where" the content of the sequences comes from, or "when," or "why." We forget that social decisions are made prior to linguistic constructions (Mehan 1972:7).

References to *productivity*, in my sense of the word, are not entirely missing from the literature, however. One teacher who has shown a consistent concern for it is Lipson. The goal of a language course, he says, is communication in a natural language environment, with the students making their own sentences motivated by a desire to communicate specific information. He chooses vocabulary that students will *want* to talk about, regardless of its rank in frequency counts. He also chooses some words not familiar to the student, or typical of his native environment, hoping in this way to *reduce the student's inhibitions* in *playing* with the content (Lipson 1971:235f). The details of Lipson's very interesting method, or even its aptness, are not of concern here. I have cited his work as an example of attention to "where" a student responds from, and "when" and "why," rather than the eternal "how."

The concept gets mentioned from time to time in the writings of others though it seldom receives sustained attention. One very useful list of productive activities is found in Rivers (1972), who remarks that "unless [the students'] adventurous spirit is given time to establish itself as a constant attitude, most of what is learned will be stored unused, and we will produce individuals who are inhibited and fearful in situations requiring language use" (78).

In their discussion of the psychological characteristics of instructional strategies, Bosco and DiPietro (1971) list eight binary "distinctive features." One of these they call "Idiographic vs. non-Idiographic." In a strategy called "+Idiographic," the student "is not forced into pre-established molds, but is encouraged to manifest expressional spontaneity"

(46). These writers examine the Grammar-Translation, Direct, and Audiolingual Methods in relation to their matrix of distinctive features. Their finding that all three are predominantly "non-Idiographic" supports my statement (above) that concern for productivity is usually submerged in our preoccupation over getting the kind of reflective behavior that we want. (Careful examination of at least one widely used "cognitively" oriented textbook by another author indicates that the same generalization may apply to this type of course as well.) Further corroboration is found in their prediction that while future strategies "will become more personalized and communication-oriented, [they] will continue to emphasize the generalized [linguistic] patterns and [cognitive] integrated processes underlying language behavior" (52). Unfortunately, the authors do not develop further the meaning of "idiographic."

The word *performance*, as it is used in this chapter, includes the meaning that it has when it is contrasted with *competence* in the writings of generative-transformational scholars. By its inclusion of "from where," "when" and "why," however, it goes beyond what those writers usually describe when they use the term.

The same is true for the word *productive*. We are accustomed to hearing speaking and writing referred to as "the productive skills," and it is indeed true that most student activity that is productive, in the sense of this chapter, will involve speaking and/or writing. But it should be obvious that speech and writing can also be reflective; Bosco and DiPietro confirm our suspicion that in organized language study they usually are.

LEARNING: DEFENSIVE OR RECEPTIVE

In Chapter II we introduced the idea of a "dimension of depth," using evidence from studies of human memory. In Chapters IV and V we tried to see what may be found along that dimension, borrowing theoretical equipment first from Maslow and then from Berne and Harris. Using this same metaphor, *productive* performance comes from somewhere *deeper* within the student than *reflective* performance does. The chapters on memory generally support the belief that, other things being equal, *the "deeper" the source of a sentence within the student's personality, the more lasting value* it has for learning the language. This carefully qualified conclusion is not likely to cause much argument. What is likely to be more controversial is a further assertion which I believe to be justified by experience if not by experiment: that this same "depth" factor, far from being an additional, minor consideration to be taken into account only when weightier factors are equal, is in fact *more to be reckoned with than technique, or format, or underlying linguistic analysis.* Here, on this page, in this paragraph you see the reason for the writing of this whole book.

"The deeper the source of a sentence, the more lasting value it has for learning a language." But an utterance can only come from as deep within the student as the student himself has allowed the language to penetrate. Performance, whether it is productive or reflective, depends on the quality of previous *learning*. There is, I think, a terribly important difference between learning that is *defensive*, and learning that is *receptive*. This is the second of the two distinctions that I said I was going to make.

Defensive Learning

"Defensive" learning sees the foreign language as a vast set of sounds and words and rules and patterns that are to be transferred from the teacher or the textbook into (or onto!) the mind of the student. In this view, the teacher—and, later on, the speakers of the language in the host country—are seen as hurling darts at the student. If a dart strikes an unprotected area (that is, if the learner makes a mistake in speaking or understanding), the experience is painful. What the learner tries to do, therefore, is to see to it that there are as few chinks as possible in his armor. Learning thus becomes a means of adapting to academic require- ments, or to life in a foreign country; but like a suit of armor it is a burden, to be worn as little as possible and cast off entirely (*i.e.,* forgotten) at the first safe opportunity. Meantime, the teacher is an adversary (at best a congenial sparring partner), against whom the learner may defend himself in a number of ways: by learning some of what he is told to learn, of course, but also by daydreaming, by ridiculing the teacher behind his back, or by damaging books and equipment associated with the course. (Much of this description of "defensive" learning is based on Curran 1966; 1972; 1968:349. Cf. also Bruner 1967:129f.)

Current writing about language teaching abounds with references to "instrumental" and "integrative" motivations. This distinction seems to me to represent one of the few important breakthroughs that I have witnessed during my professional lifetime. Thus far, however, it has remained more seminal than fruitful, honored more by citation than by

exploitation. Lambert himself has warned that in examining the instrumental-integrative dimension, we have only made a start toward understanding the motivations of a person who is studying a foreign language
(1970:94). Although "instrumental" motivation should not be tied too
closely to what I have called "defensive" learning, there is probably a
positive correlation between them. "Instrumental" motivation, characterized by "a desire to gain social recognition or economic advantages
through knowledge of a foreign language" (Gardner and Lambert
1972:14), is relatively superficial and, in the terms that we used in Chapter
IV, "analytical." Its goals therefore lend themselves to fulfillment through
piece-by-piece acquisition of items that appear to be potentially useful,
and through hour-by-hour compliance with imposed requirements.

Receptive Learning

"Receptive" learning is quite different. It is more like what happens to
seed that has been sown in good soil. In this metaphor, we may compare
language teaching to truck farming. The goal is bushels per acre: amount
of vocabulary, fluency, comprehension or structural control per man-year.
Several factors will affect the yield.

One factor is the seed. Its counterpart in language teaching is the
content of the materials, including the linguistic analysis on which they are
based. We have for many years been aware of the importance of the seed,
and have spent considerable time and money in trying to improve it. We
still have far to go, of course.

A second factor is the machinery used for cultivating the plants once
they have sprouted and begun to take root. Again, we have long been
conscious of the importance of methods and teaching aids. We produce a
steady stream (eddy?) of innovation in method, and occasionally some
careful research. (This is in many respects either healthy or necessary, and
sometimes both.)

A third obvious factor is the richness of the soil: the native
endowments which students bring with them to our training programs. A
fourth is the weather—all of the ephemeral variations that are physically
beyond our control. Meteorological weather, with its changes in baromet-
ric pressure is one example. Sprained ankles, chicken pox, family strife,
and worry about international events are others.

There are, however, at least two factors which I have not yet
mentioned. The language teaching profession has tended to lump these

two factors together with the weather, outside its area of responsibility. These are the boulders and the weeds—ego-defense reactions of withdrawal and aggression—which either prevent the seed from taking root in the first place, or very quickly choke it out. Those few writers who have looked steadily at this side of language learning are unanimous in emphasizing the importance of going back to an open, plastic, more spontaneous state that was characteristic of childhood: the soil needs to be soft and open and free. Boulders and weeds interfere with this.

No metaphor should be pushed too far, and this agricultural one has probably reached the point of diminishing returns. What I am saying is that, if we wish to promote "receptive" learning, we need to bring to our work an understanding of the ego-defenses which both student and instructor use, and of the reasons why they use them. Defense mechanisms are triggered whenever either (a) a person is not sure what are the realities of the situation in which he finds himself, or (b) he does not know how to deal with those realities in a way that satisfies him. We teachers are quite accustomed to introducing students to realities and telling them how they ought to deal with them *at the levels of attendance requirements and linguistic structure,* but realities exist *at all levels of personality.* Full "cognition" requires more than five senses and an intellect.

For the intellect never comes forth by itself, any more than blood flows independent of heart, liver, kidneys or lungs. The linguistic skills that a student gets out of some one element of a course are only the most superficial part of what that element has meant to him. (This is the point that we made at some length in Chapters IV and V.) The same element that provides practice on the present subjunctive also has significance for him at deeper levels. It is these more profound meanings that will either bind the student's personality or release it, and only insofar as the whole person is free can the part that we call "mind" turn itself to "receptive" learning of the present subjunctive or the names of the animals in a barnyard.

What we have said about "receptive" learning up to this point has been metaphorical and very general, a discussion of the conditions under which that kind of learning can take place. Before going further, we should consider the relative desirability of "defensive" and "receptive" learning.

We have already asserted that the "deeper" the source of whatever the student produces, the greater its value for retention and assimilation. We based this assertion largely on experimental studies of human memory.

If this is true, then one advantage of doing away with the boulders and the weeds is that we thereby open up greater "depths" within the student's personality. In addition, by reducing threats to the student's ego, we remove some of the occasions for playing defensive "games" of the kinds described in Chapter V. Ausubel has said, "A central task of pedagogy . . . is to develop *an active variety of reception learning* characterized by an independent and critical approach to the understanding of subject matter" (emphasis added). Rivers states that fatigue often has an emotional rather than a physical basis (1964:70).

What has come to be called "integrative" motivation, then, consists largely though not entirely of one kind of receptivity—the absence of certain types of boulders and weeds. Gardner and Lambert (1972) tell us that an integrative motivation implies "a willingness or desire to be like representative members of the 'other' community, and to become associated, at least vicariously, with that other community" (14). This in turn implies that the learner feels little or no threat from the "other" group. Lambert and a number of others have carried out a series of studies in a variety of cultural settings, all of which have supported the hypothesis that "an integrative motive, independent of intelligence and language aptitude, is important for second-language achievement" (128).

This feeling of comfort with and openness to an "other" of course applies to individual teachers, and not only in their role as representatives of alien cultures. Elliott, who teaches composition to his fellow Americans, tells his colleagues that "your job as an English teacher is to get the students to use language your way in large part as a result of wanting to, not having to, be together with you" (1970:53). Newmark long ago began to place heavy weight on the personal qualities of foreign language instructors, with an eye to promoting the kind of learning that I am calling "receptive," based on motivations that are analogous to what Lambert *et al.* have called "integrative."

The studies of contrasting "integrative" and "instrumental" motivations have been based largely on nonadult students who are studying a foreign language while resident in their native culture. Larson and Smalley, whose experience has been largely with adults in relatively small batches, have examined a process which they call *dealienation.* To some extent, going through dealienation in a foreign culture means actually doing what the "integratively" motivated student back home was willing to do but didn't need to. When a person leaves his home culture, he becomes an alien. He is then faced with a decision that is often unconscious, but nonetheless important: "Will he coexist indefinitely without ever becoming a member of this new community, or will he submit and seek to acquire the perspective of its members? Will he retire into an alien ghetto protected by imported surroundings, and choose his friends only from those who will move into *his* world, or will he learn to understand and participate in a new way of life?" (1972:3) In other words, will he both seek and accept dealienation? One possible advantage of "receptive" learning, and of fostering "integrative" motivations, may be that to do so will ease any future process of dealienation.

Receptive Learning in the Literature

The term *receptivity* has not to my knowledge appeared in the literature of language teaching. (Curran and others have used it, but they are not primarily language teachers.) There are occasional references to related concepts, but even these tend to be programmatic and very brief.

One of these related concepts is *affective*. Thus Chastain, among 15 prospective topics for future research, lists "student factors that affect achievement—in both the cognitive and affective domain" [sic] (1971:143). He does not elaborate, and the word *affect* is not to be found in the index of his book. In a later article (1975), he examines some of the variables in the affective domain, and infers that "affective factors have at least as much influence on learning factors as do ability factors."

Bosco and DiPietro, in the article cited earlier, list "± Affective" among their eight binary distinctive features for the psychological aspects of instructional strategies. A strategy is said to have an affective focus "if importance is given to motivational factors, emotional tone, value systems, and attitudes of acceptance or rejection" (45). They find the Direct Method to be (predominantly) "+Affective," Grammar-Translation and Audiolingualism to be "−Affective." They make no judgment concerning cognitive code-learning, but by the same textbook to which I referred on p. 109 it appears that this approach is no more "+Affective" than Audiolingualism is. The authors' own prediction is consistent with this inference. In an anthology titled "Toward a Cognitive Approach to Second-Language Acquisition," they assure their readers that "the gains made by linguistic science in this century will not be lost to the foreign-language classroom in favor of some vague situation-oriented instruction reminiscent of early direct-method approaches" (52).

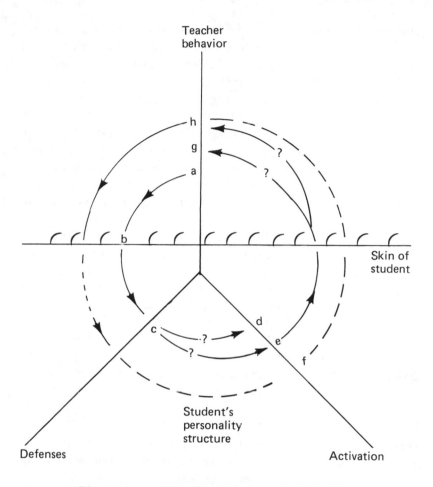

Figure 4   The "Psychodynamic Spiral"

The geometrical diagram of Figure 4 is an oversimplification of the role that the teacher can play in promoting "receptive" learning. Of the three radii, only one lies outside the skin of the student. The other two are inside it, susceptible to direct outside influence only through the use of drugs. The meaning of the diagram is as follows. The teacher typically takes some initiative (*a*) which is received by the student (*b*) and which encounters his defense system (*i.e.,* poses a threat, creates anxiety, etc.) *at* some level (*c*). This level of threat limits the depth *from* which the student will be able to act in response to the teacher's initiative, though it does not absolutely determine it: the student may act from depth (d) or (e), but not from (f). The teacher in turn continues the interaction on a level (g)-(h) which is determined partially but not absolutely by the depth from which the student acted. Thus there is a possibility for a spiral of gradually increasing radius (*i.e.*, interaction at progressively greater depth). Obviously, the spiral will not expand indefinitely, for eventually it meets with limiting factors. Some of these limiting factors will be restrictions which the culture(s) of the participants place on intimacy among occupants of a language classroom. Others, however, originate within the persons of teacher and student. Those that are parts of the teacher's actions are particularly potent because of the dominant social role that is available to him.

This is to say that the spiral will eventually become a circle, no matter how astute the teacher, or how "receptive" the student. The goal is not to replace the circle by a spiral, but to follow the spiral to a circle with the widest possible radius. Much—though not all—of the responsibility for the radius depends upon the teacher, and upon what he or she does with the options that are available (top radius in the diagram).

The radii in this diagram are obviously the by now familiar "dimension of depth." To make an impressionistic and wholly unscientific quantification, learning is probably proportional to the area of the circle; that is, it is proportional to the square of the radius.

Productivity at Various Levels

Productivity, as I have used the term in this chapter, is really a matter of making choices, which may be available at a number of different levels. In this section, we will look at some of these levels, roughly in order of their "depth" and complexity.

Least productive, in this sense, is *drill* as we used the term in Chapter V: the desired response is completely determined by teacher/textbook and the student is told when to respond.

Perhaps the simplest choice, though not necessarily the "shallowest," is the decision whether to speak at all. This choice is not limited to such specialized methods as "Community Language Learning" (Chapter VIII), or to the "free conversation" phase of more conventional styles of instruction. It becomes available in Step 3 of the simplest drill procedure, and in analogous ways of handling other types of activity. The vital difference to the student is between speaking because he has been *called on* to speak, and speaking because he is *ready* to speak.

A related kind of choice lies in deciding *when* to say or do something, whether that something is predetermined by teacher/textbook, or whether it is (partly) original with the student. This choice is available in Steps 3 to 5 of the drill procedure given on p. 79f. It is also available in self-paced activities, and may be one of the strongest features of programmed instruction.

Another general category of choice allows the student to select from a very restricted set of alternatives. Again, Step 3 of the drill procedure (p. 79) is one example. Rivers' use of "mixed drills" (1964:107) is apparently similar in intent.

Step 4 of the drill procedure represents a choice of which word to use in a specified pattern. The same type of choice appears in the "pastime" variety of exercise. In the same type of exercise and in many others, students may be allowed to choose the structure to use for a prescribed purpose. As a simple example, the teacher may instruct Student A to "ask B whether it is raining." In a drill situation, the single desired response might be for A to turn to B and say "Is it raining?" With the kind of freedom that was referred to above, A might also be allowed to say "Do you know whether it's raining?" or "It *is* raining, isn't it?" or any of a number of other things. A combination of lexical and structural options is provided by such a request as "Describe today's weather." Variations in this area of productivity are the purpose of cross-classifying questions according to their grammatical form and their relationship to a given story or dialog.

A choice which probably precedes all other choices in many genuine communicative events, but which usually is withheld from language students, is *who* to talk to in the first place. The privilege of making this choice is sometimes granted—or imposed—by the perfunctory "Ask someone whether it is raining," "Ask someone to describe today's weather," etc. The choice of an interlocutor becomes much more meaningful when it is combined with the further freedom to choose *what* one is to say. From the "productivity" point of view however, these two kinds of freedom can, and sometimes should, be separated.

Related to choice of what to say is choice of how to structure an ambiguous situation. This kind of freedom is complex enough and important enough to deserve multiple illustration. One common type of ambiguous situation is a picture, about which the students are invited to invent one or more stories. Even the clearest photograph contains some ambiguity. Pictures which are less representational, or even abstract, provide still more leeway for the student's imagination, and more opportunity for investment of his self.

Another well known source of ambiguity is the role-playing assignment: "Jones, take the part of the bookseller, and Smith, take the part of the customer." (The degree of ambiguity can be reduced by giving more detailed instructions.) One interesting variant of this technique is to give partially conflicting instructions to the participants, with neither knowing the details of the other's intentions: "You are a bookseller who has just received a large shipment of very expensive dictionaries that you want to get rid of," and "You go to a bookstore to buy an inexpensive pocket dictionary." (This technique is taken from observation of Japanese classes supervised by Eleanor Jorden at the Foreign Service Institute.)

Still another type of potentially fruitful ambiguity may be found in literature that is profound enough to express general human truth. How might one, for example, write a contemporary paraphrase of Hamlet's "To be or not to be..."? One group of English teachers, considering this question, found a striking parallel in an episode through which their country had just passed—in a dramatically un-Hamletlike way. Other people, or the same people at another time, would have come up with another solution.

In ambiguous or openended situations, some of the alternative responses involve less emotion, and some involve more. The wording of an assignment may therefore call for varying degrees of "productivity" at this level also. A class, studying *Flowers for Mrs. Harris* by Paul Gallico, might be instructed merely to "Describe Pamela Penrose." The same lexical and structural practice would be provided by the "deeper" "What do you like about Pamela Penrose, and what do you dislike about her?" Or, "If Pamela Penrose were your sister, what would you say to her?" In providing "comprehension questions" over a reading about plastic surgery in World War I, one might ask only the neutral "Did G. at this time know much about plastic surgery?" and "What operation did S. describe in his writings?" Or one might include some questions that call for judgment and feeling: "Is plastic surgery the least important branch of medicine?"

"Which would be worse, to lose your right arm, or to lose your lower jaw?" "How much would you pay to have your left ear replaced?" This sort of question, with its visceral implications, goes far beyond routine testing of "delayed recall from long-term memory," yet it makes no greater linguistic demands on the student.

Also at a relatively deep level is the choice of how much risk to take. In a purely linguistic context, this choice begins to become available already in Step 3 of the drill procedure (p. 79). Here, in doing uncued recall of the sentences of the drill, the student may try something that he is not quite sure of, or he may stick with something with which he feels more secure.

Risks can be especially meaningful—and therefore "productive"—when they relate to content and to potentially emotional issues. The teacher who has his class practice the sample addresses and phone numbers in a textbook is calling for none of this kind of risk. To use the addresses and phone numbers of students themselves is to ask for confidential information which they may or may not be ready to reveal to one another. Even the answers to Wilson and Wattenmaker's "What do you see in this room that you like?" (1970) may elicit a wide range of responses from the same person, depending on the level of trust.

In summary, we should "judge creativity in the classroom by what the teacher makes it possible for the student to do," (Strasheim 1971:345) and not just by what the teacher does.

This rather lengthy discussion has documented my earlier assertion that "productivity" is not an all-or-none characteristic of a classroom event. This section has also related "productivity" to the "depth dimension," and through it to the concept of receptive learning.

A PSYCHODYNAMIC INTERPRETATION

We turn now to what, for want of a better term, we may call a *psychodynamic* interpretation of what happens in language classes. The Greek term "psychodynamics" translated into Latin would be something like "intra- and inter-personal action," and in plain Anglo-Saxon "what goes on inside and between folks." The Anglo-Saxon, as usual, is the most direct and expressive way to put the matter; unfortunately, there is no convenient way to make an adjective of it. In any case, and in whatever language, we shall base this formulation on all that has preceded it in this book, and we shall test it in the chapters that follow.

First, we focus our attention on two principles that underlie foreign language *learning.*

A Psychodynamic Interpretation of Language Learning

Principle Ia: Language is one kind of purposeful behavior between people. Obviously, this is not a definition, but only a partial description, in which the key words are *purposeful* and *people.* It shifts emphasis away from the audiolingualists' "Language is a system of oral symbols . . ." and beyond the more recent view of language as "creative, rule-governed behavior" (Chastain 1971:88). It uses the "system" for a purpose, and it "creates" for a purpose, and these purposes inevitably involve other people.

Principle Ib: And language behavior is intertwined with other kinds of purposive behavior between people. Even in the earliest weeks of infancy, the interaction between child and mother reflects "a rather finely tuned and potentially meaning-laden system wherein each allows the other to act" (Lewis and Freedle 1973:128). From that stage on, except in language classes, people ordinarily do not talk without having something to say to someone else. But even in language classes, people do not communicate by words alone. Tone of voice, body language, and many other channels carry *at all times,* wil-we nil-we, messages that either confirm the words, or are irrelevant to them, or contradict them. Lozanov makes a major point of this observation when he talks about the "biplanarity" of communication; his method develops "biplanar" communication, based on scientific principles, into a fine art (p. 43).

Principle IIa: The human mind learns new behavior rapidly at any age. This says neither that the mind learns with *equal* speed at all ages, nor that the learning process at age 20 is pedagogically or physiologically the *same* as it was at age 2.

Principle IIb: But (many kinds of) learning will be slowed down when the learner is busy defending himself from someone else. In Maslow's theory (1970), the highest form of motivation is "self-actualization," and this can be realized only when threats on all preceding levels have been reduced to tolerable amounts. In Berne's theory (1972:Ch. 5), the optimum "way of structuring time" is "intimacy," a "candid, game-free relationship, with mutual free giving and receiving and without exploitation" (Berne 1972:25). Some degree of intimacy is a precondition of receptive learning. The writings of Curran, Gattegno and Lozanov, unlike the writings of most of us full-time career language teachers, make the reduction of defenses into a matter of fundamental importance and chronological priority (cf., Libit and Kent 1970:55). One of the most fascinating aspects of comparing methods (Chapters VIII, IX, X) is to see how differently this problem is dealt with by various practitioners.

Innumerable writers have listed innumerable principles of foreign language learning. To omit them here is not to say that those principles are invalid, or even that they are unimportant; it is however to say that the two listed here are, from a psychodynamic point of view, central.

Placing "principles of learning" before "principles of teaching" is consistent with the ideas of Gattegno (1972), Wardhaugh (1971:19) and some others, even though it conflicts with the practice of many.

A Psychodynamic Interpretation: Foreign Language Teaching

From a psychodynamic standpoint, the central principles of language teaching are also two in number.

Principle III. Help the student to stay in contact with the language. This principle, like Principle IIa, is as important for what it does not say as for what it does say. In the light of Principle I, staying in contact with the language means more than merely listening to or looking at sentences in the language, even if one understands their meaning. The teacher/textbook must ordinarily maintain the student's understanding of the language: in the terminology of Principle Ib, they must keep clear how the language strand of behavior is related to the other strands. But Principle Ia says that behavior is not only a cable, it is also a cable that is attached at both ends: the teacher must help the student to maintain interpersonal purpose on one or (preferably) more of the levels that we have listed (p. 49f). Goals differ in range (short or long) as well as in level.

Principle IV. Help the student to maintain wholesome attitudes. With some simplification and a little distortion, we may state the national mottos of Audiolinguia and Cognitia as follows:

> Audiolinguia: "The crucial (though not the only essential) factor in second language learning is the quantity of oral activity."
>
> Cognitia: "The crucial factor in second language learning is the quality of mental understanding."

In contrast to these formulations, the present chapter says:

Terra Incognita: "The crucial factor in second language learning is the quality of personal activation."

This is a point at which the teacher's whole personality makes an impact, of course. This is where the teacher may try to supply missing motivations, whether "instrumental" or "integrative" (Prator 1971). This is where a relatively mechanical procedure like Interaction Analysis (Moskowitz 1968, 1971, 1974; Krumm 1973) may provide the raw material for invaluable insights into the effects of one's teaching behaviors. Here, too, in watching oneself in a videotaped microteaching episode, one may profit from turning off the sound.

But this is also the point at which technique comes into its own, both for minimizing frustration and confusion, and for avoiding a feeling of stagnation in class activity. And this is where advances in linguistic analysis may cast light on the whole process, from writing of materials, through planning of lessons, all the way to teaching in the classroom. As guidelines for employing technical virtuosity in a more "psychodynamic" way, we may suggest the following:

1. *Reduce "reflectivity."* Even theoretically, reflectivity cannot be reduced to zero, for the student inevitably requires at least brief exposure to a suitable model. It is even doubtful whether it should be reduced as far as possible, for to do so might produce destructive anxieties at other levels. Nevertheless, many of the tribal customs widely practiced in all major styles of language teaching are unnecessarily reflective.

2. *Increase "productivity" at as many levels as possible.* The meaning of this injunction is illustrated on pp. 116-119.

3. *Teach, then test, then get out of the way.* The maxim "teach, then test" has long been known to us. A fair paraphrase is probably "present the new material clearly, so as to develop a new bit of 'competence'; then conduct some activity which will enable you and the students to verify that this competence has indeed become available as a basis for performance." Insofar as this formula has reminded us not to confuse "teaching" and "testing," it has served a useful purpose. Unfortunately, however, it has often been subjected to a particular kind of distortion, which has changed it from a

moderately helpful principle into a pernicious one. The distorted version is: "Teach, then test, then teach some more, then test some more, all the way to the end of the course." In the metaphor of p. 115, this application of the rule produces a circle of small radius. In some of the terminology of Chapter V, it tends to perpetuate the Controlling Parent—Adapted Child nexus. It tends to minimize "productivity" and maximize "reflectivity." If the personalities of teacher and students are such that learning becomes partially "receptive," the depth of the "receptivity" is nevertheless limited to the relatively shallow level from which "productivity" is accepted. In teaching and then testing, the teacher is fulfilling essential Natural Parental functions: (1) meeting the fundamental security need by providing structure and continuity for the student's activity, and (2) serving as a link between the neophyte and the demands of the foreign language. By failing—or even refusing—to get out of the way, the teacher becomes a Controlling Parent. Just how often to "get out of the way," and how soon, and how far, are matters of judgment which cannot be prescribed here or in any other book. In general, however, most of us would do well to step farther aside, and sooner and more often, than we are accustomed to doing. As the teacher learns to limit himself, he can give more independent meaning and value to the others in the classroom (Curran 1968:213).

A Psychodynamic Interpretation of Materials Development

Principle V. In preparing materials, make it easy for teacher and students to follow Principles I-IV. Affirmatively, this means providing potentially purposeful material (*cf.,* in my 1971 treatment, "occasions for use," "samples," "social and topical dimensions," and especially "strength") that will minimize confusion (*cf.,* "transparency" and guided "exploration") and forestall stagnation (*cf.,* "lightness"). Negatively, it means refusing to use the materials as a showcase for technical virtuosity beyond the demands of the first four principles.

CONCLUSION

These five principles make up a set of correlative assumptions about the nature of language and the nature of language teaching and learning. We might therefore, using Anthony's figure of speech (1963), say that they represent an *approach* to our subject matter. In another metaphor, they are simply a way of looking at our work, just as the infrared camera brings out features of an aerial photograph which do not appear on conventional film.

How is this way of looking at language teaching related to recent calls for greater emphasis on "communication," and to exhortations that we take into account the affective side of education? First, I have tried to explore "what happens inside and between folks in a language class" more thoroughly and more systematically than hitherto. Although what I have done is only preliminary and very tentative, I have drawn a rough map rather than just mentioning a few landmarks.

Second, the point of view set forth here contrasts with the idea that "communication" is one of three indispensable stages, following "mechanical" and "meaningful" practice, or that "depth" is reached only after a series of preliminary steps. I have tried to see the personal and interpersonal significance of mechanical and meaningful practice, as well as of genuine communication, at all levels in the "depth dimension," extending from the first minute of instruction to the last.

In the chapters that follow, we shall look at several methods— successful methods—that appear on the surface to be quite different from one another. We shall view them through the "psychodynamic" filter of this chapter, to see whether in this chapter we have, indeed, found some of the underlying principles to which they all conform.

VIII
Community
Language Learning

Special thanks are due to Daniel Tranel, who read the first draft of this chapter and made numerous very helpful comments. Final responsibility for errors of fact, interpretation or emphasis, remains, however, with me.

In 1957, when most speech correction was directed at fairly specific isolable problems, Backus (1957:1036) viewed speech in psychological terms for everyone, and not just for those with so-called speech disorders. She sought the causes of speech behavior in interpersonal relationships. Her strategy derived from the belief that the reduction of barriers is of more basic importance than presentation of content or acquisition of skills in speaking (1061). Accordingly, she tried to choose situations in which clients could actively participate with ease and pleasure, and in which the therapist could help them to discover what is expected (the limits imposed) while at the same time showing permissiveness, warmth and acceptance (1055).

Community Language Learning (CLL), which is the subject of this chapter, follows a very similar approach. The purpose of this chapter is to describe the basic procedure of CLL, and then to see how it exemplifies or fails to exemplify the five principles set out at the end of Chapter VII. Further information about CLL may be found in Bégin (1971), Curran (1961, 1968, 1972), LaForge (1971, 1975), and Stevick (1973).

A DESCRIPTION OF COMMUNITY LANGUAGE LEARNING

The basic procedure of CLL has two main steps: *investment* and *reflection*. In the investment phase, the learner commits himself, as much as he is able and willing, as he engages in a conversation with other members of the learning community. In the reflection phase, the learner stands back and looks at what he, as a part of the community, has done in the investment phase. As he does so, he remains a member of the community.

Permeating both phases is the dimension of student security. At the beginning, the student typically has numerous negative feelings. Some of these feelings may come from pre-existing prejudices toward speakers of the language being learned, or from earlier bad experiences with language in general. Others may arise directly out of the learning situation itself. Not the least source of insecurity in the beginning of any language course is the student's total ignorance of the language. As the process of community learning goes on and these negative feelings are dealt with, and as the student begins to become familiar with the language, the student's role changes in the direction of greater and greater security and independence.

In addition to the learners, there is at least one resource person, who knows the language being learned, who also understands the native language of the learners, and who has some expertise in a nondirective style of counseling.

Mechanically, the procedure is uncomplicated: the learners, seated in a closed circle, simply talk with one another in the foreign language, tape-record what they say, play it back, write it down, and identify its component parts. The resource person stands outside the circle. None of these details is essential, however. They are merely one method of making possible the communication out of which community may grow. The chief immediate motive for communication is the need to belong.

According to the degree of independence that the learner shows at a given time, he is said to be in one of five *stages.* In the investment phase, a student in Stage 1 says aloud, in his native language, whatever he wants to say to another of the learners. (In the beginning, the sentences should be kept short.) The resource person then stands behind that learner and, speaking close to the learner's ear, supplies the translation. The style in which this help is given is one of the crucial elements of the procedure. The resource person's voice must sound clear, but also gentle and supportive. If the learner makes an error so serious that it must be corrected, the resource person may supply the phrase again, but in a voice that is totally free of disapproval or reproach. The student holds the microphone of the tape recorder and switches it on just long enough to put onto tape his own words in the foreign language. Then it is someone else's turn to continue the conversation.

A student may elect to say the sentence first in the foreign language, without waiting for help, and then give the native language equivalent. Whenever he does so, he is said to be in Stage 2. A student is in Stage 3 when he speaks directly in the foreign language, giving a native-language translation only if someone requests it. In Stage 3, the learner is enjoying his newly won ability in the language, but becomes annoyed or discouraged if he is corrected often. Since a student in Stage 3 is still making numerous errors, this stage is a trying time for the resource person whose native language is being frequently distorted. In Stage 4, the learner has developed enough security so that he can accept, and even welcome, corrections from the resource person without being thrown off stride. In the fifth and last stage, the learner's use of the foreign language is basically correct, so that the resource person is free to suggest nuances of vocabulary and structure which make the learner's speech more elegant or idiomatic.

The reflection phase consists of three steps. First, immediately after the period of investment, the students talk about the experience in its cognitive, but also in its emotional and physical, aspects: the whole person has an opportunity to express itself at this time. The resource person listens to whatever is said and reflects it back, in the learners' native language, in an understanding and noncritical way. He neither agrees nor disagrees with the learners, nor tries to give them information or answer their objections.

The second step in the reflection phase consists of playing back the recorded conversation without interruption. This step takes very little time, since a conversation which took five minutes to record may last only 20 or 30 seconds when all the pauses, native-language originals, and voicings by the resource person have been omitted.

In the third step of this phase, the conversation is played back again, this time sentence by sentence. In one version of this step, the sentences are written on the board, and the learners make their own copies. Each learner supplies the translations of the sentences for which he was responsible. The resource person then helps the learners to identify individual words, prefixes, suffixes, etc. This ends the basic procedure. The learners are now ready to begin recording a new conversation.

COMMUNITY LANGUAGE LEARNING AND THE PRINCIPLES OF CHAPTER VII

Principle I. Language is purposeful behavior between people, intertwined with other kinds of purposive behavior between the same people. The first conversations recorded during the investment phase often consist of cautious and somewhat erratic small talk: "It's a nice day," "Have you seen any good movies recently?" and the like. Here, the principal purpose may be to satisfy the requirements of the new and unfamiliar CLL format. But after a few times through the basic procedure, including the first step of the reflective phase, students begin to feel more secure. As this happens, they begin to talk—during the investment phase—about things that are really on their minds. (Sometimes this includes their opinions of CLL, or of each other.) They invest more and more of themselves in the content of what they say, thus fulfilling Principle I to the extent that is hard to match in the beginning level of more conventional styles of instruction. The learners are always "enacting themselves" (Jakobovits and Gordon 1974:72); and the wish of Jakobovits and Gordon (1974:31) to "*begin* the teaching of a language at the ... level [of ordinary communicative interactions]" is realized.

Principle II. The human person learns new behavior rapidly if the learner is not busy defending himself from someone else. As we said earlier, the "someone else" may be the teacher, or a former teacher; it may be one or more fellow students, or all fellow students; it may be specific foreigners who speak the language being learned, or the learner may have feelings of fear, resentment or contempt against all speakers of that language—or even against foreigners in general.

Aside from negative feelings of the kinds mentioned in the preceding sentence, Curran believes that the very disparity of knowledge between the teacher (who knows, in effect, everything) and the student (who knows little or nothing) usually requires some sort of emotional adjustment on the part of the student.

Community Language Learning deals with these potentially destructive reactions in at least four ways. The first, chronologically, is the behavior of the resource person during the investment phase of the first three stages. This person remains outside the circle; he stands behind the person he is helping at the moment, and therefore is invisible to that person; he uses a very reassuring tone of voice, which implies understanding of what the learner is going through; he speaks gently, but close enough to the learner's ear so that he is within the learner's personal space, so that the foreign sounds almost seem to the learner to originate within his own head; he does not tell the learners what to say, but only how to say it; he neither criticizes nor praises. If the resource person is sufficiently skilled as a knower-counselor, the learners will forget that he exists as a separate person. At the same time, he provides them with all the linguistic support they ask for.

The second way in which CLL reduces defensiveness is found in the first step of the reflection phase. Here, the learner has an opportunity to voice directly whatever the investment phase has brought to his mind, and to have these thoughts understood without evaluation, comment, or questioning. This experience, in itself, often has a healing effect.

As time goes on, and the learners begin to talk about more than trivia, they have an opportunity to hear—and to overhear—one another under the safe conditions described. This is a third way in which the need for self-defense is reduced.

Finally, in the later steps of the reflection phase, the taped record of the investment phase is entirely in the voices of the students. Even the written record is, as far as possible, made in their own handwriting. This further minimizes confrontation of the learner by an overpowering knower.

One may question whether this kind of learning will not produce another, and even more disturbing, kind of insecurity in the learners. After all, the content of what is said, plus its tape-recorded and written manifestations, has come from them. The person who is supposed to lead them, and in whom they need to have confidence, is inconspicuous, and has even tried to become a non-person in their eyes.

A parallel question may be raised with regard to the resource person. How long can he continue to be only a tool, or a foreign-language reflector, in the hands of the learners? What satisfactions are available to him, to compensate for the lost roles of "originator" and "judge"?

To some extent, the objections outlined in the preceding paragraphs rest on an incomplete understanding of the role of the resource person. First of all, this role is one which must be chosen consciously and accepted willingly. It is not without its responsibilities and its rewards. This person does, after all, provide and maintain the basic structure of Community Language Learning. He still does point out salient features of grammar. He does continue to provide ancillary activities and materials outside of the basic procedure described in the first part of this chapter. He even makes some corrections, especially in Stages 4 and 5. So the learners are not really left completely to their own devices, particularly in the very fundamental decisions about format of instruction.

On the other hand, it is true that the resource person in CLL must do without the "originator" and "judge" roles that are so much a part of other styles of teaching. He must be able to draw deep satisfaction from watching the learners develop through the five stages. He must be patient with small linguistic imperfections in Stages 1 and 2, and with larger ones in Stage 3. He must be more concerned about what the learners can and will do in the language than about how they perform on the usual kind of discrete-point test (Jakobovits and Gordon 1974:87, 104; M. Sommer, personal communication).

Principle III. Help the student to stay in contact with the language. We have already seen, in discussion of Principles I and II, how the learner in CLL works with a form-meaning complex in which the meanings are very much his own, and in which the forms are presented in a way which is least likely to cause him to break off contact with them.

Principle IV. Help the student to maintain wholesome attitudes. Again, the discussion of Principle II has already given a general picture of how CLL meets this requirement. In our original discussion of Principle

IV, we suggested three general guidelines for selecting techniques that would contribute toward wholesome attitudes:

"Reduce reflectivity." CLL complies both by leaving content up to the learners, and by putting the spoken and written models into their own voices and handwriting as soon as possible. (Note that *reflectivity* is used here in a sense different from the "reflective" phase of CLL.)

"Increase productivity at as many levels as possible." If *productivity* means "generating language in which one has exercised choice," then CLL is clearly in keeping with this guideline.

"Teach, then test, then get out of the way." In CLL, some of what goes on in the last step of the reflective phase may look like an attenuated form of what we generally think of as "teaching." There is no "testing" in any usual sense of that word. Of course, CLL is far beyond other methods in meeting the "get out of the way" part of the requirement. The absence of conventional testing will bother some teachers and even some students, who will ask, "But how am I to know what grade I've earned? How will I know my standing in the class?" For such teachers and students, CLL fails to meet one of the five criteria of Chapter VII. It is probably also true that for those people CLL will not work. But for teachers and students who are able to paraphrase the "test" part of this guideline as, "How do my performance in the language and my ideas about its structure stack up against the realities of the language?" the alternation of reflection (especially the last step) and investment provide a deeply satisfying alternative to the traditional kind of test (*cf.*, Jakobovits and Gordon 1974:49-57).

Principle V. In preparing materials, make it easy for teacher and students to follow Principles I-IV. Students who are engaged in CLL do have access, outside of class, to conventional grammar books and, as I hinted above, ancillary procedures are sometimes used in the class session itself. But the only "materials" used in the basic procedure are the tape recordings of the conversations, and daily digests of the sessions prepared and distributed by the resource person. These materials help to prevent the successive rounds of investment and reflection from degenerating into a formless mess in the learner's mind.

OTHER OBSERVATIONS ON COMMUNITY LANGUAGE LEARNING

In the terminology of Transactional Analysis (Chapter V), CLL recognizes that the learner comes to any new course of study with many characteristics of the Child: ignorance, insecurity, self-centeredness, dependence or rebelliousness, and so on. On the other hand, the facts about any new language are Parent data *par excellence*: externally imposed and inescapable prescriptions about how things always have been and are supposed to be. In most steps of the basic CLL procedure, the resource person, operating in his own Adult, nevertheless presents himself to the learners as an understanding and all-sufficient Nurturing Parent, without the officiousness or the well-meaning interference of the Controlling Parent. If the resource person limited himself to this function, however, most learners would probably stay in Stage 3 forever, and after leaving the course would either speak a permanently distorted form of the language or suffer a lifelong case of lathophobic aphasia. Here, I suspect, is the crucial function of the first step of the reflective phase. In this step, conversation is in the native language of the learner. The Child-Parent relationship made necessary by the foreignness of the new language is suspended. The resource person, as a sympathetic, understanding, nonjudgmental listener, lends his Adult objectivity to the learners. The learners may begin in Parent or in Child, but by accepting the loan of the resource person's Adult they more readily enter their own Adult. Having done so, they are more able to welcome suggestions and corrections, and so to make the crucial transition from Stage 3 to Stage 4.

I have used Transactional terminology in an attempt to provide a different perspective on CLL. This should not, however, be taken to mean that the therapeutic principles of Transactional Analysis are identical to those of Counseling-Learning, from which CLL is derived.

Because of its therapeutic aspects, CLL seems to be particularly effective with students who have studied the language in a traditional course for a year or more but who cannot make active use of it (LaForge 1975).

Since my review of Curran (1972) was published, I have used CLL with real classes in three languages, and colleagues at the Foreign Service Institute have used it in several others. Also, I have received firsthand reports of its use by three other teachers on three continents. The results have been linguistically very successful and, from a psychodynamic point of view, quite exciting. My conclusions at this writing are twofold. First, the basic procedure itself seems to be sound enough and sturdy enough to survive use by teachers who know it only second- or third-hand. Second, the crucial step is the first part of the reflective phase, where the resource person listens to the reactions of the students. This must be done in a way which shows understanding and acceptance, but which does not try to answer the students, or to approve or disapprove of what they have said. In large-scale use of CLL, the importance of this step becomes even greater. To do it successfully requires a skill for which most people require special training.

Since completing this chapter, I have greatly increased my own experience with Community Language Learning. It can be much more varied in its procedures than the above discussion indicates. Moreover, it is only one special case of a broader approach, to which the name "Counseling-Learning" is sometimes given. "Counseling-Learning" is not so much a collection of ideas as it is a full and integrated personal commitment on the part of the teacher. I urge anyone who is attracted by Community Language Learning as a method to become familiar with the thinking that underlies it, either through first-hand exposure, or through reading Curran's printed works.

IX
The Silent Way

The greater part of this chapter consists of a review of the second edition of Gattegno's *Teaching Foreign Languages in Schools: The Silent Way.* I regret that this description of the Silent Way is fragmentary and in no sense authoritative. I believe, however, that it is sufficient to show how the principles of Chapter VII may be applied to this unconventional method. Those principles are:

I. Language is one kind of interpersonal behavior, and it is intertwined with other kinds of interpersonal behavior.
II. The human mind learns new behavior rapidly at any age, provided the learner is not busy defending himself.
III. Help the student to stay in contact with the language (in the sense of Principle I).
IV. Help the student to maintain wholesome attitudes.
V. In preparing materials, make it easy for teacher and students to follow Principles I-IV.

SOME BASIC FACTS ABOUT "THE SILENT WAY"

Like Curran, whose work we looked at in Chapter VIII, Caleb Gattegno does language teaching as a by-product and special case of a professional commitment which is broader than language teaching as such. Again like Curran, Gattegno makes almost no mention of those who are conspicuous in the field; in turn, his own published works are cited only rarely in our books and journals. The first edition of his book received no serious reviews in the United States, and as far as I am aware, the second edition has thus far been entirely ignored by other reviewers.

It is not hard to understand how this has happened. I found the first chapter of the first edition so annoying that I refused to read further. I find the second edition exciting and utterly charming from cover to cover, but this fact is probably due less to the differences between the editions than it is to five intervening years of hit-and-run—or hit-and-miss—encounters with the Silent Way in practice. This review, therefore, while centering on the book, necessarily reflects my total experience with what strikes many of us as a bizarre way of learning and teaching.

My first view of the Silent Way was in a brief demonstration, which I found good but not memorable. I did not begin to take it seriously until a year later, when I watched an actual Spanish class in its seventh hour of instruction. That session was one of the most impressive I had ever seen, not only for the amount of language that the students controlled but also for the variety and intensity of the personal energies that were released. A year later I attended a two-day seminar on the Silent Way. From that time on, although I was by no means "sold" on the method, I began to pass on bits of it to teachers with whom I worked in various parts of the world. The responses of these teachers and their students, even to these second-hand fragments, were so positive that I gradually came to reexamine my own thinking. Meantime, I saw a number of demonstrations—some of them outstanding—by other people. I have seen the method used brilliantly in a class of one person, and in a class of 70. Most recently, working in partnership with Turkish instructors who had had no previous experience with the Silent Way, I took a beginning class through their first 150 hours, using little except rods and purposive silence. This, then, is a summary of the background out of which I write this review.

Gattegno's commitment is to solving some of the problems of learning in general; for him, teaching foreign languages is only one special case of broader principles which he has also applied in teaching mathematics, and the reading and writing of the mother tongue. Accordingly, his first chapter sets forth some of those ideas. The five that seem to me most important, both for understanding this book and for the illumination of any style of teaching, are the following:

1. *Teaching should be subordinated to learning* (1).

2. *Learning is not primarily imitation or drill* (3). This, a key tenet of post-audiolingual methodologists, was present in the 1963 edition, at a time when audiolingual orthodoxy was at its height. In this respect, Gattegno's thinking runs parallel to that of Curran (1968:344ff), who sees learning in relation to the total and changing value-structure of the learner. Drill is valuable, he says, only insofar as it is substantially tied in with the personality of the learner. As we shall see below, the Silent Way gives primary attention to the social forces at work in the class.

3. *In learning, rather, the mind "equips itself* by its own working, trial and error, deliberate experimentation, by suspending judgment and revising conclusions." (4) Here, a year before *Games People Play*, is an almost verbatim description of the "Adult" ego state (Berne 1964:24 *et passim*, Harris 1967:50ff) together with an affirmation of the importance of this ego state in the learning process.

4. *As it works, the mind draws on* everything it has already acquired, particularly including *its experience of learning its native language* (12). For Gattegno, therefore, the differences between first- and second-language learning loom larger than the similarities, so that he is content to devise an "artificial" method (12), rather than trying for a "natural" one.

5. If the teacher's activity is to be subordinate to that of the learner, and if the learner's activity is to be of the kind described in 3 (above), then *the teacher must stop interfering with and sidetracking that activity* (13). Here is the principal reason for the silence which gives this teaching its name. At the same time, this frankly artificial approach is, in some respects, very strictly controlled (12). The teacher provides knowledge of the language and a firm overall structure for activity. In so doing, he meets a part of the student's deep need for security (Maslow 1970:39), and fulfills the role of a

Nurturing, or Natural Parent (Berne 1972:13, 118). At the same time, however, he avoids the constant modeling, prescribing and directing kinds of activity which are typical of the Controlling Parent (*ibid.*), and which many teachers seem to believe are inseparable from effective, responsible teaching. But this allegation on my part calls for a description of how the Silent Way is used.

Anyone who has ever heard of the Silent Way at all knows that it makes use of a set of *rods*, which are small wooden blocks of ten different lengths but identical cross-section, each length having its own distinctive color. In addition, a fully developed set of materials contains a word chart, a phonic chart in which phonemic distinctions appear as contrasting colors, drawings, worksheets, and several books (15).

With regard to the linguistic units themselves, the basic strategy of the Silent Way agrees with many other methods of the past 30 years, by concentrating first on the acquisition, within a small vocabulary, of control over pronunciation and the structural elements (Fries 1947:3). Chapter 3, which many readers will see as the central chapter, is titled "Much Language and Little Vocabulary."

THE FIRST LESSONS

In a typical first lesson, the vocabulary begins with "a rod" and goes on to such expressions as "a blue rod," "a red rod," etc., ending with the imperative form "take. . .". The teacher pronounces each new input very clearly. Ideally, a new input should be given only once, but in any event the students get only what they absolutely require. From the very first minute, the students do 90% or more of the talking, while the teacher remains almost completely silent. At all times, speech is accompanied by appropriate action (generally consisting of manipulation of the rods), and action is accompanied by appropriate speech. The method thus has one of the characteristics which the "Total Physical Response" experiments showed to be so desirable for establishing durable comprehension (Kunihara and Asher 1965; Asher 1974).

But this first lesson has two additional strong points which are seldom found elsewhere. The first of these points is related to what we are discovering in research on short-term memory. According to one widely accepted view (*e.g.*, Mayor 1969:1165; Nelson 1971:565; Norman 1970:2; for a recent alternative interpretation, see Craik 1973), new auditory material is retained for about 20 seconds in a state in which it is available for inspection and even rehearsing, something like a loop of tape, or like a small worktable on which bits of new and old material may be assembled, sorted and rearranged. This is the reason why human beings are able to "do a doubletake" in response to something they heard a few seconds earlier. But if further new auditory material is introduced into short-term memory before the first material has faded from it, the later material will interfere with the person's ability to process and assimilate the earlier. Silence, on the other hand, gives the mind maximum opportunity to extract information from a short bit of aural input. In most of our methods, the barrage of utterances from teacher and fellow students is like a handful of stones thrown onto the surface of a quiet pond: we are unable to follow the ripples from any one of them becuase of interference produced by the others.

It is for this reason that, in my own attempts to use the Silent Way, I have learned to forbid *any* immediate repetition of new material spoken by the teacher. The enforced silence that surrounds the new words both allows and compels maximum attention and superior processing. The first individual or group production of this material comes about three seconds later (well within the span of short-term memory), in response to a fresh presentation of the visual stimulus. If one student does not get it right, he is given more time and some nonverbal help. If he still does not get it, others are silently invited to try, and the best version is indicated by the teacher—again silently. Then (in a small class) the rest of the students may produce the utterance, each in response to a fresh stimulus.

This use of silence means that the student derives much more benefit per audible model from the teacher. It might be argued that even if, in comparison to other, noisier ways of teaching the student absorbs 10 times as much *per model* from the teacher, the noisier ways still produce a greater effect in the long run if they provide 50, or 25, or even just 11 times as many models:

If L(earning) = N(umber of Models) $\times$ B(enefit per Model)

$$B_S = 10\,B_C \qquad\qquad N_S = \frac{N_C}{X}$$

Then L_c is greater than L_s if X is greater than 10. I find, however, that this argument leads to a conclusion that does not square with my observations. The reason, apparently, is found in a fundamental difference between two ways of looking at the mind of the student. In one view, it is a clay tablet on which lines are engraved by patiently scraping a cutting tool over the same line until the desired depth is reached. In that view, the silence of the Silent Way has the effect of softening the clay so that fewer reiterations are necessary. Gattegno's view, as we have already seen, is quite different. He sees the mind as an active agent, capable of constructing and refining its own "inner criteria." In the former view, "whenever a student makes a mistake he is practicing a mistake" (the cutting tool is being drawn over the wrong part of the tablet), and "practice of any form makes that form more likely to be used in the future." Therefore we must insist on "accuracy before fluency." These, of course, are dogmas of a comparatively unenlightened version of behaviorally oriented audiolingualism, so much maligned of late. By contrast, Gattegno tells us that "to require perfection at once is the great imperfection of most teaching." Teacher and student alike must be "shaken loose a bit from their timid perfectionism" (Levertov 1970:167) if anything creative is to take place.

The concept of "inner criteria" (14, 28) finds a close parallel in Titone's discussion of "linguistic feeling" (1970:60). Titone also seems in general accord with Gattegno on the route that leads to this kind of mastery: through incorporation of basic patterns, followed by inference of the basic rules through observation and deduction, rather than through mere grammatical theory.

Gattegno's view of the mind places him very clearly in what today we may call the *cognitivist camp.* (It is interesting to remember that he occupied this position in 1963 and, in fact, much earlier.) Indeed, both in his theory and in his practice, he places much greater faith in the mental powers of even the ordinary student than does any other cognitively oriented system with which I am familiar. As one colleague put it after 28 hours of a beginning course, "This was a little hard at first but then it became easier as I learned to use my mind in ways that I had forgotten were available to me." Or, in Gattegno's words (25), language learning may become "a recovery of the innocence of our self, a return to our full powers and our full potentials."

This leads to the second of the two strong points that I mentioned above: the resources which the Silent Way makes available for helping wholesome things to happen inside, and between, the people in a classroom. Compared to this, teaching with rods and a minimum number of repetitions is merely an interesting *tour de force*, and the efficient use of the power of short-term memory is superficial. The student who was relearning to use her mind in ways that she had forgotten was growing in self-awareness; a student who can say "I have learned" rather than "I have been skillfully taught" is developing self-respect. Words written by a poet teaching poetry describe also the aim and effect of the Silent Way: "My hope was not to teach anybody . . . but to attempt to bring each one to a clearer sense of what his own voice and range might be, and to give him some standards by which to evaluate his own work" (Levertov 1970:147).

The interpersonal implications begin to show themselves already, in the first few lessons, in at least two ways. I have a 20-minute demonstration of the method—or at least of my best understanding of it—which I have used with numerous audiences. During that period, I open my mouth only seven times, each time to pronounce one word. After each of these inputs, I shape the learners' production by a process of selective reinforcement, with results that are at least as good as what one gets through massive "mimicry"-memorization. At the end of the demonstration, the learners are producing, without prompting, any of nine simple three-word phrases. I then stop and ask an open ended question: "What happened?"

One of the most frequent answers, and often one of the first, is "We learned how much we could depend on ourselves and on each other," or "We felt that we were working together as a group in relation to you." Nor is this reaction confined to the first few minutes. I recently interviewed a class that had completed about 180 hours of instruction, most of it by our best approximation of the Silent Way. One of the things these students said first and most firmly was that the method offers exceptional opportunities for them to help and be helped by one another, and that they place great value on that aspect of it.

Even the fact that the imperative "take" appears in the first lesson is helpful for intragroup relationships. Using this form, the students are able to interact directly with one another, with visible and verifiable *but nonverbal* responses. The language that one student chooses to use does not force his fellow students to produce further language if they are not ready to do so.

Another feature that regularly receives comment, both in the early stages and later on, is that the students' attention simply does not wander even after six or more hours a day. Still another is the absence of destructive competition: when the students are depending on one another, the unique contributions of each are clearly recognized and valued by all, for even the slower students will, from time to time, remember something or figure something out that has escaped the others.

These, then, from the psychodynamic view, are some of the respects in which the Silent Way shows rich possibilities.

But as with any other method, students come up sometimes with a right answer and sometimes with a wrong one. What then? In the case of a correct response, the answer to this question is simple but unorthodox: the student must learn to do without the overt approval of the teacher. Instead, he must concentrate on developing and then satisfying his own "inner criteria." This means that the teacher is supposed to react never verbally and seldom nonverbally to a correct response. There is none of the "very good!" or the enthusiastically nodding head that many authorities tell us we should produce on these occasions. Indeed, some practitioners whom I have observed come across as stern and almost gruff. Others seem to manage a "warm, sympathetic and understanding" style without giving explicit approval to right answers. (I suspect that the desirable compromise is to show pleasure as a person rather than approval as a judge.) From the Transactional point of view, teachers may thus reduce the Parental component of their behavior (Berne 1972:104). In so doing, they presumably evoke less of the Adapted Child in the student (Berne 1972:104), and therefore clear the way for the flourishing of an Adult-Adult relationship.

What is usually called a "mistake" seems to have unusual significance for the silent teacher. The student who made the mistake has "stuck his neck out," acting vicariously for the whole group. The content of the mistake itself is an invaluable clue to where the students are in the development of their "inner criteria," and so it provides precious guidance for the teacher's next step. There are many ways in which the teacher may respond. Choice among these ways, in Gattegno's view as I understand it, should conform to two principles: (1) Remain silent if at all possible. (2) Give only as much help as absolutely necessary. In the early stages, use of hand signals, colors, etc. may form an elaborate and detailed system for locating places where the inner criteria need further work, or even for indicating what the desired response is. These devices still have the advantages of requiring/permitting the student to provide the answer on at least the auditory level, and of keeping all students' auditory short-term memories uncluttered. But if the teacher continues this sort of help beyond the time when it has become superfluous, he is interfering again, and students will grow restless as they feel their "learner space" invaded (Curran 1972:91).

Although silence on the part of the students is not a goal of the Silent Way, a certain amount of it may occur under these circumstances. LaForge (1971:57) found the silences of Community Language Learning (a system quite different from the Silent Way) to be periods of intense and valuable mental activity. Levertov (1970:175) recognized that toleration for silence, when it does occur, may be at the same time both a result and an expression of confidence in oneself and in the other members of the group. Of quite specific relevance to the uses of silence is a recent report of research on one facet of verbal memory.

In experiments reported by Buschke (1974), subjects were required to learn lists of 20 nouns. They were then asked to recall as many words as they could, in any order. They were allowed to try each list as many times as necessary. Before each trial, they were re-exposed *only* to those words which they had not yet recalled on their own during a previous trial. At each trial, unlike many of the other list-learning experiments that have been reported, the subjects were encouraged to take their time, and to continue trying past the point where recall became difficult.

Four of the observations that came out of the experiment were the following: (1) Most of the items that failed to be recalled on some one trial "were retrieved later without any further presentation, indicating that such failures represent retrieval failure rather than loss from storage" (579). (2) "Once an item was spontaneously recalled after previous recall failure, it usually was consistently recalled thereafter" (580). (3) The fact that it is possible to retrieve additional items by extended recall is something that must be *learned* (581). (4) "Subjects in the experiment reacted positively to the challenge of achieving their own maximum retrieval without further presentation" (581).

"TEACH, THEN TEST. . ."

In Chapter VII, we drew a three-way distinction among "teaching," "testing," and "getting out of the way." One advantage of the Silent Way, it seems to me, is that it lends itself exceptionally well to keeping these three kinds of activity separate from one another: when the teacher is both making the noises and moving the rods, he is "teaching"; when he is moving the rods and expecting the students to make the noises, he is "testing"; when he leaves both the rods and the noises up to the students, he is "out of the way." Furthermore, in the Silent Way the teacher spends much less time in the "teaching" mode than in other methods that I have seen.

There still remain, of course, questions of how and how long to teach, how and how long to test, and how long to stay out of the way. A final advantage of the Silent Way is that, not being required to keep the classroom filled at all times with audible language, the teacher has more opportunity to observe the students' performance and modify his own actions accordingly—what Gattegno calls being "with" the students.

SOME GENERAL QUESTIONS

I shall not describe the rest of the Silent Way in as much detail as the first lessons, partly because of limitations on my personal experience with it. I believe, however, that the first lessons contain those features of the method which are at the same time crucial to it and most characteristic of it. But there remain two frequently asked questions which demand attention here.

1. *Isn't the value of the Silent Way largely confined to the early stages, for teaching numbers, colors, spatial relations, and a few things like that?* Having taken one class successfully to 150 hours primarily by my best approximation of this method, I can only reply in the negative. This must certainly be the answer if we think of the Silent Way as a way of looking at teaching and learning, rather than as a set of operations with rods. But even from the latter point of view, the answer is still "no." In fact, numbers and colors are, in my opinion, among the least interesting uses of the rods, because for these purposes the rods are most easily replaceable by other devices.

2. *How essential are the rods, really?* For years, I was skeptical on this point, preferring to use toy villages, or Tinkertoys, or real objects, and actively refusing to have anything to do with rods. I now prefer rods to Tinkertoys because they are more visible, less distracting, come in more colors, and do not roll off the table.

My reasons for preferring rods to toy houses and cars are more important. (1) The representational objects tell the beholder what *kind* of house, school, etc. to see: they preempt the functioning of imagination, which is one part of the total personality that we are trying to activate. (2) It is hard for representational objects to become what they are not. Rods, by contrast, have unbounded flexibility. The same rods may become, now a map of the Middle East, now a picture of a traffic accident, now a graphic analog of the surface structure of the Turkish noun, now a visible record of information that a student is giving about the neighborhood in which he lives. At the more advanced levels, students seem to appreciate the shared concrete record of what they are talking about. As Maria del Carmen Gagliardo says in an appendix to the book (132), the rods are both "austere" and "mesmerizing."

CONCLUSION

This book has an inescapable personal flavor about it. I think it would not be improper to make two observations in this regard.

One quality that comes across on many pages is the author's humility and sense of humor. He recognizes that his experiments have been limited in scope (2), and that his conclusions "may not be universally valid" (43). He has a quiet chuckle at his own expense in citing ways in which he exemplifies his observation that "strange uses of the language are common among learners who choose to be at peace within themselves rather than bow to the traditions of the foreign language" (24).

But along with this humility—perhaps growing out of it—we find an unbending loyalty to whatever light the author has been able to find (xi). He has been granted to see parts of the truth that no one else had seen before him (vii). He refuses to dilute or alter the distillate of his experience in order to make it more palatable to others. He believes that, at best, all he can hope to educate in us, his colleagues, is awareness (x). Both in this method and in this book about the method, he is consistent with his principle of maintaining the integrity of what is to be taught and at the same time enhancing the integrity of the learners (52). It is as though he is saying to us "Once you have understood this for yourself, you will have no further need of me. And if I tried to give you a clue at the cost of your own experience, I would be the worst of teachers" (Herrigel 1971:76). Again in conformity with this principle, he withdraws the promise, made in the first edition, to provide a Teacher's Manual.

Although this review has been frankly favorable, I do not intend it as a blanket endorsement either of the book or of the method which it describes. Some few parts of the book are open to serious question from the point of view of standard linguistic science. More important, it is frequently tantalizing in the questions it raises or in the partial answers it gives. As for the Silent Way itself, I have not seen enough of it in action to regard it as the one methodological pearl of great price; it is, however, possibly the most undervalued pearl on the market today.

* * *

We turn now to an examination of how the Silent Way conforms or fails to conform to the principles set forth in Chapter VII. The presence, visibility, and manipulability of the rods mean that words are always intertwined with other kinds of interpersonal behavior. The rods are, moreover, flexible enough to parallel many different kinds of verbal behavior, whether that behavior is explaining a new point of grammar, or practicing that point in a systematic way, or telling a story, or playing a game. Students therefore remain in contact with the entire form-meaning complex at all times. Nor is this merely a theoretical feature of the Silent Way: it is, in fact, one of the features most frequently mentioned by the students with whom I have talked.

The above observations related to Principles I and III, which I said described the content of a psychodynamically sound course. Principles II and IV have to do with matters of attitude and emotion. Most people who use the Silent Way expect to keep the student under fairly constant tension. The total security of the first three stages of Community Language Learning (Chapter VIII) is missing; in Curran's terminology, learners in the Silent Way are assumed to start out in Stage 4. When the

Silent Way is used at a fast pace, students commonly feel overwhelmed, abused, and without hope. How then can this method possibly comply with Principles II and IV? Surely the student will be thrown so much on the defensive that his learning capacity will be severely impaired! And, surely, the attitudes that grow out of feeling overwhelmed, abused and hopeless will be anything but wholesome!

In fact, however, students do not react in these ways. There are apparently at least three reasons why this is so. First is the atmosphere of solidarity and cooperation among the students, which the method produces from the very beginning (see above, p. 145). Another is the mesmerizing quality of the materials and the procedures (above, p. 145). A third, and perhaps the most important, is a phenomenon which has been recounted to me by so many different people, in so nearly the same words, that I cannot think it is unrelated to the method itself. After a few hours, when the frustration and tension had become almost intolerable, these people report a sudden metamorphosis in their feeling, and a shift to serene and happy learning of a kind that they had never before experienced. One may speculate that this metamorphosis depended to some extent on the partial successes of the hours that preceded it, and to some extent on the profound realization that this terrifying and unreasonably demanding teacher was both competent and on their side (Stevick 1974:380f). I am fairly sure that there are other factors as well. In any event, once the metamorphosis has taken place, there is no longer anyone from whom the student needs to defend himself. On the positive side, he sees himself making unbelievably rapid progress as he works with his own inner criteria and (re)discovers his own full potential as a learner.

Here is the point where the principles of Chapter VII would predict that the Silent Way would fail. The method may, of course, be taught in a low-pressure way, with good success and little risk. But if it is taught at full speed, the student must experience the metamorphosis or he will be defeated. This may happen for reasons rising from his own background, or because the teacher has for some reason failed to gain his confidence.

As for the materials, they are Spartan in their simplicity, with everything pared away which does not contribute toward the student's development of his own inner criteria.

X
Some Other Methods

THE SAINT-CLOUD METHOD

A method which has received considerable attention in recent years is variously known as the Saint-Cloud Method, the CREDIF Method, and the Audio-Visual Method. The following discussion is based principally on its treatment by Renard and Heinle (1969).

The Saint-Cloud Method certainly takes into account the first principle stated in Chapter VII: that "language is purposeful behavior between people, intertwined with other kinds of purposeful behavior between the same people." Renard and Heinle are clear that "nonverbal . . . behavior is . . . essential in communicative interaction, and forms an integral part of the presentation of language-in-use" (11). "Language is . . . an acoustic-visual [whole]: the situation cannot be separated from the elements that constitute its linguistic expression" (12). "Language-in-use" is a combination of an expressive and communicative purpose, and a formal linguistic structure, and the purpose of the Method is to teach language-in-use (12). Even structural manipulation in this method takes the form of questions and answers because this simulates actual communication and thus "requires language to perform its social function" (14). The pictures and the many kinds of questions which the teacher asks, mostly about the picture, are intended to maintain a combination of meaning with form—to keep the student in contact with the language" (Chapter VII, Principle III).

Principle II, that people learn best when they are not busy defending themselves, is less conspicuous. But the authors quote Guberina and Rivenc, the originators of the method, that the French people and their language must appear to the student "as little intimidating as possible" (viii). Renard and Heinle also refer briefly to "the limited amount of research" on the effects of various characteristics of the person who is serving as model, and of the person who is observing and imitating that model (10).

Principle IV recognizes the desirability of "helping the student to maintain wholesome attitudes." In this respect, it seems to me that the greatest strength of the Saint-Cloud Method lies in the very fundamental area of "security" (Chapter IV). A teacher who has had the prescribed training course, and who uses the materials as they were intended to be used, will always know what he is doing, and what he is going to do next, and why. Similarly, his students will always feel that their learning endeavors are receiving firm and dependable guidance. On the level of "esteem" (Chapter IV), the constant stream of question-answering and repetition after a recorded model, if carefully guided by the teacher, provides opportunities for progressive satisfaction resulting from a growing facility with the language.

The Saint-Cloud Method—a method with many successes to its credit—thus complies to some degree with the four principles which we have quoted from Chapter VII. This is of course a vindication, not of the method, but of the principles. I believe, further, that these same principles can illuminate some of the limitations of the method. This is particularly true if we take into account the dimension of depth, or the concept of the whole person.

This method, as we have quoted its practitioners above, correctly emphasizes that what is to be taught is "language-in-use," which consists of a form-meaning composite. But in its concern to make all of the meanings clear through pictures, it limits (except in the very last part of the last phase of each unit) the meaning to the fixed, and therefore dead, world of the filmstrips. What is happening in almost the entire unit, then, is not "having lunch"; it is, rather, "talking about someone on the filmstrip having lunch, using vocabulary and structures that we may someday need while actually having lunch." Even the very final step (Renard and Heinle 74f) usually has the students acting out situations that the teacher has already outlined for them. There appears to be little room for investment that is drawn from the nonacademic parts of the student's personality.

Furthermore, a method in which students spend almost all of their time either answering questions or repeating after a tape is bound to be highly *reflective,* as I have used that term in Chapter VII. For most of the time, whatever creativity the student exercises and whatever choices he makes are under careful control of the method and the classroom teacher. When students are finally allowed to "behave a new but related situation" (74), they do so at the end of a long series of gradually relaxed controls.

The features which make the Saint-Cloud Method so very "reflective" also place the students in a parallel—or competing—relationship with one another relative to the teacher. All are trying to do the same thing, and it quickly becomes clear which ones are doing it better than others.

The last few paragraphs have been descriptive, but also critical, of the Saint-Cloud Method: we have said that it restricts students, both in the spectrum of reality about which they talk, and in the areas within their own personalities which may contribute to creative personal investment in the learning process. We have implied that it has within it relatively meager opportunities for satisfaction of the needs for "belonging" and "self-actualization" (Chapter IV). How can such a method be successful?

No method is always successful, of course. I am acquainted with at least one adult who was destroyed as a learner of French by the constant barrage of questions, and the judgmental manner of the teacher, in a course taught by this method. Early in the course, failure to give back specific items correctly was expanded and institutionalized into a pattern of overall failure. The only possible source of reassurance—the teacher's approval—was thus cut off. This style of instruction minimizes the interpersonal dynamics among students, which in the methods of Chapters VIII and IX provide alternative sources of support.

But the method often does work. When it does, the reasons are probably of two kinds. First, some students are able to survive and even to thrive (cognitively at least) in the kind of atmosphere we have described.

These are students whose mistakes in the first lessons are few enough so that they are not withered by the teacher's disapproval; whose imaginations are suggestible enough and vivid enough to bring to life the two-dimensional filmstrips; whose needs for security, clear structure and teacher approval are more urgent than their needs for group support or for immediate relevance; who are happily Adapted Children (Chapter V) when the teacher acts as their Controlling Parent. There are many such people, and in many parts of the world they represent the cultural norm for the role of Student.

The Saint-Cloud Method may also succeed because individual instructors provide an atmosphere which contains elements not called for by a literal reading of the procedures: unconditional personal acceptance by the teacher, group spirit among the students, opportunities for greater personal investment and a wider range of creativity.

This method, then, like most other conventional methods but unlike the methods of Chapters VIII and IX, subordinates learning to teaching, and teaching to materials. The materials are, however, worked out with unusual care, thoroughness, and ingenuity.

LANGUAGE TEACHING AS APPLIED LINGUISTICS

One idea most widely circulated among language teachers during the past 25 years is that their work is, in some important sense, a branch of applied linguistics. The most essential qualification of a foreign language teacher is the ability to "diagnose . . . students' areas of linguistic interference, to design appropriate [materials based on this information], and to plan programs keyed to the problems of the individual" (Morray 1975:5). This point of view could be documented from dozens of sources, but we will look in detail at only one: "Calm or chaos in the classroom," by Lois McIntosh (1974). Although this article is brief, and was not intended by its author to be a major theoretical work, I have chosen it for four reasons. It is recent; it is clearly written; it is, in my opinion, an authentic statement of some widely held ideas; its theme of "calm or chaos" relates more directly to the major themes of this book than do most presentations of similar ideas.

As I understand the article, its argument is as follows: In our concern about linguistics and psycholinguistics, we should not forget the student. The student is entitled to a chance to work calmly, and free from external disturbances. If the teacher makes inept or irrelevant attempts to be entertaining or sociable, or if she shows favoritism, chaos results. We produce chaos if, in correcting an error, we at the same time put down the person who made the error. Chaos may also result, however, if the teacher fails to understand the problems which the target language presents to the learner. Almost the entire article is devoted to this last sort of chaos. "Calm" results when the teacher recognizes and understands the learning problems and knows what to do about them.

If I understand McIntosh correctly, "chaos" as used here might be paraphrased as "anxiety and threat." In this interpretation, it is interesting to examine the article in terms of Maslow's hierarchy (p. 49f). Viewed in that light, this article seems to be principally concerned with the "security" level of need, which is the most fundamental one, and with one part of the "esteem" level. That is to say, it places its main emphasis on the well trained, well organized, neat and friendly teacher whose class hums along smoothly and without awkward pauses. The student's esteem need is satisfied by a steady stream of successes in dealing with the sounds, grammatical patterns, and vocabulary of the new language. There is no real recognition of the kinds of "chaos" that come from unsolved problems of group membership, either within the classroom or on an intercultural scale (p. 55). Nor do we read about the kinds of reward that can come from the subordination of teaching to learning—from the student's discovering *how* his own mind can work for him, rather than merely totting up *how much* the well trained, well organized, neat and friendly teacher has taught him.

If "chaos" is "anxiety and threat," then "calm," its opposite, must be "security." And if this is so, then "chaos" in the sense of "apparent lack of complete organization" would not be incompatible with "calm." And if the students are putting into the course more of themselves than just their disembodied intellects, then a certain amount of this second, superficial kind of "chaos" is desirable. The McIntosh article, like the school of thought that it represents, makes no real allowance for this latter kind of chaos, or for the student self-investment that is one of its sources.

So this approach, like the audiovisual approach discussed earlier in this chapter, works, but it works (a) with students who are able to suspend many of their needs other than those for security and for approval for purely linguistic achievement; and/or (b) on a very shallow basis which leaves the students unable to transfer readily what they have learned to the demands of real-world language use; or (c) because an individual teacher or a class has gone beyond what is recommended in McIntosh's article, and dealt with the full range of needs.

Relative to the principles of Chapter VII, this article recognizes that study should take place in a meaningful context, but it seems to see the main purpose of behavior in the classroom as being to learn and practice plural endings, tense sequences, and interdental fricatives. It emphasizes strongly that students should be spared the need to defend themselves, but it is incomplete in the range of potential threats which it recognizes. The "language" with which it places the student "in contact" is externally imposed, sanitized material carefully arranged to avoid the kind of "chaos" with which the article is mainly concerned. And, in its care to avoid one type of unwholesome attitude, the article overlooks the development of a whole range of wholesome ones.

AUDIOLINGUALISM

The so-called audiolingual approach, in one or another of its many forms, has held the center of the stage for most of the time since World War II. In recent years, of course, it has come under increasing criticism. My purpose here is neither to attack it nor to defend it, but only to look at it alongside the principles of Chapter VII. As with all the other methods examined in Chapters VIII-X, I recognize that it has met with great, but not uniform, success.

For the purpose of this discussion, I shall draw primarily on the expression of audiolingualism set forth in the Teacher's Manuals for Level One (Modern Language Materials Development Center 1961). This is neither the latest nor the fullest exposition of this approach, but is perhaps the most widely circulated.

Looking at the principles of Chapter VII in reverse order, a conspicuous feature of audiolingualism is that while the teacher makes a clear distinction between "teaching" and "testing" (1961:123), he almost never "gets out of the way." At most, the better students may be invited to ask the [sic] questions over a narrative (1961:26), and at one point in the use of response drills, students are encouraged to reply *to the teacher* using as much variation of vocabulary and structure as possible (1961:22). Relatively free conversation is limited to four or five minutes per day, closely based on situations suggested near the end of each unit (1961:24). There is thus a great deal of "reflectivity" (Chapter VII), and "productivity" (*ibid.*) is severely limited. All errors should be corrected immediately

(1961:3, 17, 21, 26), and the student should be neither required nor allowed to figure things out for himself (1961:28, 32). In treating of individual differences between students, the book recognizes only variations on learning speed and accuracy (1961:34).

In helping the student to maintain wholesome attitudes, then (Principle IV), audiolingualism makes the same assumption that we found in the approaches discussed earlier in this chapter: that the student's needs are for security and for a feeling of (purely academic) achievement. It works well with students for whom this assumption is true.

As for keeping students in contact with the form-meaning composite that is language, audiolingualism sets the learner to work on prefabricated and neatly packaged meanings presented primarily as words of the native and target languages. Learners for whom these meanings can come alive will have a chance to do well in an audiolingual course.

If the learner is a whole person with aspects that are often "physical," "mental" and "emotional," then the picture of the learner which one would get from this book has no emotional side, and even very little mental responsibility. It is true that the learner is not supposed to repeat anything that he does not in some literal sense understand (1961:13), but mastery is to be measured by what the student's speech muscles do (1961:33).

THE WORK OF GEORGI LOZANOV

At the present time, very little is known in most western countries about the work of Georgi Lozanov. What I have been able to learn about it, however, has convinced me that his findings and his methods are an essential part of the picture that I have tried to sketch in this book. The main part of this chapter is my own tentative summary, based on reading and a few videotapes. Peter O'Connell has worked carefully through one translation of Lozanov's major book on Suggestology and Suggestopedia, and has talked with a number of people who are knowledgeable in this area. He has generously permitted me to draw on a summary which he prepared for another purpose. The account which follows is presented with our joint apology for its inevitable prematurity and incompleteness, and in the hope that it will lead readers to seek later, more authentic, accounts of this very original approach to education. The best English language sources of information on Suggestopedia in the teaching of languages are by W. Jane Bancroft (1972a, b).

Some of the basic ideas behind Suggestopedia were mentioned in Chapter III (p. 42f). Lozanov uses a wide variety of means to get around the antisuggestive barriers and help the students to achieve the childlike openness, plasticity and creativity that are characteristics of what he calls *infantilisation.* The most conspicuous of these, and the most widely publicized, are the decoration, furniture and arrangement of the classroom, and the use of music. But Lozanov himself points out that these features of the method are nonessential. By far the most important elements lie in the behavior of the teacher, and particularly in the maintenance of an air of authority—confidence in self, the materials and the method, but also in the student—which engender a corresponding confidence on the part of the student—both in the teacher, materials and method, and in self. Here, if anywhere, lies the secret of the Lozanov method, and not in the description of overt procedures which follows.

The materials consist principally of ten dialogs. Each dialog has its theme, which is broken up into subthemes. Some other apparatus follows each dialog. There are also tests, which serve pedagogical as well as evaluative purposes. Each of the 10 units contains 150 new words, all of which are introduced in the context of the dialog. The class meets three hours per day. Each unit is studied for one-half of one day, all of the following day, and half of the day after that—a total of six hours of class time.

The first day begins with contact with the director. He offers certain information and advice, but the most important purpose of this initial contact is to establish in each student a feeling of confidence.

At the outset, each student is given a foreign language name, and a fictitious, prestigious occupation. The purpose of doing so is to provide the student with a mask, or shield, behind which he is safe to develop as he likes, and to make mistakes without personal jeopardy.

The first day of work on a new unit begins with a few minutes of explanation of the content (not the language) of the dialog. Then the students receive the dialog, perhaps 1200 running words of it, which is printed with a native-language translation in a parallel column. During the first reading of the text the teacher answers whatever the students want to ask about. This obviously transmits information. Moreover, the information comes at a time when the students' questions show that they are ready for it. Equally important, however, and characteristic of the method as a whole, the questions are answered in order to reduce anxiety about the information. They are asked and answered in the native language, presumably to avoid the stress and tension of a class where all talking is supposed to be in the target language.

In the second reading, the students do not follow the printed text. Instead, they sit comfortably in armchairs and listen as the teacher reads the dialog in a special way. The precise ways of using voice quality, intonation, and timing are apparently both important and intricate. I have found no one who could give a first-hand account of them.

The third reading, again by the teacher, is accompanied by carefully selected classical music. Again, the students are seated in their armchairs, in a state of "concert pseudo-passivity." But Lozanov emphasizes that Suggestpoedia is not "relaxopedia," and that it does not depend on altered brain-wave patterns or states of consciousness.

These three readings make up the presentation phase, and occupy the 1½ hours at the end of one day. The remaining 4½ hours spent on the unit are devoted to various kinds of exploitation of the dialog. My limited information on the subject indicates that the activities of the exploitation phase are not, in themselves, anything that other language teachers would consider to be out of the ordinary. The results which the method reportedly achieves, however, are definitely not ordinary: expressed in terms of vocabulary, Lozanov's students learn hundreds of words in less time and with less fatigue than our students need for 50 words. In terms of fluency, suggestopedically trained students are more ready to use what they know.

Because my picture of Suggestopedia is only second- or third-hand, analysis according to the principles of Chapter VII must be tentative. The following is at least a guess.

Principles I and III (Chapter VII) have to do with the kind of contact that the student has with the language. *Language*, as the term was used in Chapter VII, is a complex consisting of both form and meaning, it is interpersonal behavior, and it is intertwined with other forms of interpersonal behavior.

In this sense, compared with Community Language Learning (Chapter VIII) or the Silent Way (Chapter IX), Suggestopedia is relatively conventional. Its principal materials are a series of long dialogs, which apparently do not differ greatly from the dialogs of many other courses, except that they are longer. Suggestopedia thus does not produce the relatively full self-investment of the student in the materials that we find in Community Language Learning. It also lacks the constant support of the visual channel that the rods and charts of the Silent Way provide.

On the other hand, Suggestopedia does provide each student with a fictitious identity and life history. In these borrowed roles, the students can interact freely and creatively with the teacher and with one another. Videotapes that I have seen show students joking with one another, entertaining one another, and resolving differences of opinion. These are the kinds of result the conventional, but longer, nonsuggestopedic courses aim for but only sometimes achieve.

In technique, too, the best videotapes that I have seen look surprisingly like more conventional methods at their best. The suggesto-pedic principles are not, for the most part, realized as a set of obvious gimmicks. It would seem that they show up, instead, as carefully coordinated modifications of style in using existing techniques: the overt—and mostly verbal—plane of behavior must be supported by the less conscious—and largely nonverbal—plane. Together, these kinds of behavior must create an atmosphere in which the student can place complete trust, first in the teacher and then in his own powers—truly an example of the intertwining of many strands of interpersonal behavior! This, at least, is my understanding of "doubleplaneness" and "authority" in Lozanov's writing.

This brings us to Principles II and IV, which have to do with the psychic state of the learner. Here is where the theoretical and experimental basis of Suggestopedia is much more fully elaborated than we find with any other system of language teaching, and here lies, in my opinion, its most distinctive and its most interesting contribution. Suggestopedia, like Counseling-Learning (Chapter VIII), tells us that once doubts and defenses have been removed, nothing can stop a learner who has the usual extrinsic motivations.

SUMMARY: WHAT I HOPE FOR IN A CLASSROOM

In Chapters VIII, IX, and X, we have looked at a few of the many methods that are available to a language teacher. As the years go by, I find myself less concerned with *which* method has been chosen for a particular class, and more interested in *how* it is being used. I am particularly aware of what I see when I look at students and teacher.

Students

1. I hope to find the students involved in whatever they are doing, contributing to it and getting satisfaction from it on many levels of personality.

1. That is to say, I hope *not* to find them concentrating on merely coming up with correct responses (even in a structure drill), or on grinding out correct sentences or free conversations just for the sake of grinding out correct sentences or free conversations.

2. I hope to find the students comfortable and relaxed, even in the midst of intense intellectual activity or vigorous argument.

2. (a) This does *not* mean that they are loafing on the job. In fact, students who are really comfortable with what they are doing are less likely to loaf. (b) This also means that the students are not apprehensive that they will be punished if they fail to live up to the teacher's expectations.

3. I hope to find that the students are listening to one another, and not just to the teacher. I also hope that they will be getting help and correction from one another, and not just from the teacher.

3. This means that the students are *not* like separate lamps plugged into a single power supply, in such a way that the power used by one diminishes the voltage available to the rest.

Teacher

4. The teacher is in general control of what is going on.

4. This does *not* mean that everything the students do comes as a direct response to a specific cue from the teacher.

5. The teacher allows/encourages/requires originality from students, whether in individual sentences, or in larger units of activity, or in choice among a range of techniques.

5. This does *not* mean anarchy or chaos.

6. One of the first things I notice is whether the teacher seems relaxed and matter-of-fact in voice and in manner, giving information about the appropriateness or correctness of what the students do, rather than criticizing or praising them.

6. The teacher does *not*, either by word or by unspoken message, say to students, "Now always remember...," "You shouldn't have forgotten...," "You are a good/poor student," or "Now try to do this so that I may judge you on it."

These six points imply that the function of "originator," so often a monopoly of the teacher, is shared, though not to such a degree as to make the students insecure. The same is true for the function of "evaluator." Teacher and students are aware of what is going on cognitively, but also on other levels. No one, on the other hand, is haunted by what he or someone else thinks *ought* to be going on. There is evidence both of self-confidence, and of confidence in the other people in the room. And all of these things may happen, or fail to happen, with any of the methods I have described. So, of the three subjects of this book, Memory is a by-product of Meaning, and Method should be the servant of Meaning, and Meaning depends on what happens inside and between people.

Bibliography

Abel, Ernest L. 1971. Marihuana & memory: acquisition or retrieval? *Science* *173*:1038-1040.

Allen, H. B. and R. N. Campbell 1972. *Teaching English as a Second Language: A Book of Readings*. New York: McGraw-Hill.

Anisfeld, M. 1966. Psycholinguistic perspectives on language learning. In Valdman (ed.) 1966.

Anthony, E. M. 1963. Approach, method and technique. *English Language Teaching* *17*:63-67.

Asher, J. J. 1965. The strategy of the total physical response: an application to learning Russian. *IRAL 3*:292-299.

Asher, J. J., JoAnne Kusudo, R. de la Torre 1974. Learning a second language through commands: the second field test. *MLJ 58*:24-32.

Atkinson, R. C. and R. M. Shiffrin 1968. Human memory: a proposed system and its central processes. In K. W. and J. T. Spence (eds.) *The Psychology of Learning and Motivation* Vol. II. New York: Academic Press.

Bachman, J. G. 1964. Motivation in a task situation as a function of ability and control over the task. *J. Abnormal and Social Psychology 69*:272-281.

Backus, Ollie 1957. Group structure in speech therapy. In L. E. Travis (ed.) *Handbook of Speech Pathology*. New York: Appleton-Century-Crofts.

Bancroft, W. Jane 1972a. The psychology of Suggestopedia or learning without stress. *The Educational Review.*

———. 1972b. Foreign language teaching in Bulgaria. *The Canadian Modern Language Review 28*:9-13.

Barondes, S. H. 1970. Multiple steps in the biology of memory. In Quarton *et al.* (eds.) *The Neurosciences,* 1970 edition, 272-278.

Barondes, S. H. and H. D. Cohen 1968. Memory impairment after subcutaneous injection of acetoxycycloheximide. *Science* 556-557.

Baumbach, Jonathan (ed) 1970. *Writers as Teachers/Teachers as Writers.* New York: Holt.

Bégin, Y. 1971. *Evaluative and Emotional Factors in Learning a Foreign Language.* Montreal: Bellarmin.

Benne, K. D., L. P. Bradford, Ronald Lippitt 1964. The laboratory method. In Bradford *et al.* (eds.) 1964.

Bennis, W. G. 1964. Patterns and vicissitudes in T-group development. Chapter 9 in Bradford *et al.* (eds.) 1964.

Benson, D. F. and N. Geschwind 1967. Shrinking retrograde amnesia. *J. Neurol. Neurosurg. Psychiat. 26*:127-135.

Berne, E. 1964. *Games People Play.* New York: Grove Press.

———. 1972. *What Do You Say After You Say Hello?* New York: Bantam.

Bever, T. G. and R. J. Chiarello 1974. Cerebral dominance in musicians and nonmusicians. *Science 185*:537-539.

Bjork, R. A. 1970. Repetition and rehearsal mechanisms in models for STM. Chapter 10 in Norman (ed.) 1970.

Blubaugh, J. A. 1969. Effects of positive and negative audience feedback on selected variables of speech behavior. *Speech Monographs, 36*:131-137.

Blumenthal, A. L. 1962. Contributions of psychology to the language and language learning program. In Lambert (ed.) 1962.

Bogoch, Samuel 1968. *The Biochemistry of Memory, with an Inquiry into the Function of the Brain Mucoids.* Oxford Univ. Press 1968.

Borden, R. C. and A. C. Busse 1925. *Speech Correction.* New York: F. S. Crofts & Co.

Bosco, F. J. and R. J. DiPietro 1971. Instructional strategies: their psychological and linguistic bases. In Lugton, R. C. (ed.)

Bower, G. H. and Winzenz, D. 1970. Comparison of associative learning strategies. *Psychonomic Sciences 20*:119-120.

Bradford, L. P., J. R. Gibb, K. D. Benne (eds.) 1964. *T-Group Theory and Laboratory Method.* New York: Wiley.

Braud, W. G. 1970. Extinction in goldfish: facilitation by intracranial injection of RNA from brains of extinguished donors. *Science* 1234-1236.

Brierly, J. B. 1966. Some aspects of the disorders of memory due to brain damage. In Richter (ed.).

Brown, M. 1968. *A.U.A. Language Center Thai Course,* Bangkok: A.U.A. Language Center.

Bruner, Jerome 1967. *Toward a Theory of Instruction.* Cambridge: Harvard Univ. Press.

Bugelski, B. R. 1962. Presentation time, total time, and mediation in paired-associate learning. *J. Exp. Psych. 63*:409-412.

Buschke, H. 1974. Spontaneous remembering after recall failure. *Science,* 3 May, 579-581.

Carroll, John B. 1966. The contributions of psychological theory and educational research to the teaching of foreign languages. In A. Valdman (ed.) 1966.

———. 1968. Memorandum: on needed research in the psycholinguistic and applied psycholinguistic aspects of language teaching. *Foreign Language Annals* 1:236-238.

Ceraso, J. 1967. The interference theory of forgetting. *Scientific American* 117-124.

Chafe, W. L. 1973. Language and memory. *Language 49*:261-281.

Chastain, Kenneth 1971. *The Development of Modern Language Skills: Theory to Practice*. Philadelphia: Center for Curriculum Development.

———. 1975. Affective and ability factors in second-language acquisition. *Language Learning 25*:153-161.

Ciccone, D. S. 1973. Massed and distributed item repetition in verbal discrimination learning. *J. Exp. Psych. 101*:396-397.

Coles, Robert 1971. *The Middle Americans*. New York: Atlantic–Little, Brown.

Craik, Fergus I. M. 1973. A levels of analysis view of memory. In Pliner *et al.* (eds.).

Craik, Fergus I. M. and R. S. Lockhart 1972. Levels of processing: a framework for memory research. *JVLVB 2*:671-684.

Curran, Charles A. 1961. Counseling skills adapted to the learning of foreign languages. *B. Menninger Clinic 25*:78-93.

———. 1966. Counseling in the educative process: a foreign language learning integration. Unpubl.

———. 1968. *Counseling and Psychotherapy: The Pursuit of Values*. New York: Sheed and Ward.

———. 1972. *Counseling-Learning: A Whole-Person Model for Education*. New York: Grune and Stratton.

———. 1974. Lectures at a Counseling-Learning Institute, Sinsinawa, Wisconsin.

Darley, C. F. and B. M. Murdock 1971. Effects of prior free recall testing on final recall and recognition: *J. Exp. Psych. 91*:66-73.

Deese, J. 1959. Influence of inter-item associative strength upon immediate free recall. *Psychological Reports 5*:305-312.

Deutsch, D. 1970. Tones and numbers: specificity of interference in immediate memory. *Science* 1604-1605.

Deutsch, J. A. 1971. The cholinergic synapse and the site of memory. *Science 174*:788-794.

Diller, K. 1971. *Generative Grammar, Structural Linguistics, and Language Learning*. Rowley, Mass.: Newbury House.

Earhard, M. 1970. Individual differences in subjective organization: short-term memory. *Psychonomic Sciences 18*:220-221.

Elliott, George P. 1970. Teaching writing. In Baumbach (ed.).

Ellis, N. R., D. K. Detterman, D. Runcie, R. B. McCarver, E. M. Craig 1971. Amnesic effects in STM. *J. Exp. Psych. 2*:357-361.

Ervin, F. R. and T. Andrews 1970. Normal and pathological memory: data and a conceptual scheme. In Quarton (eds.) *The Neurosciences*. 163-175.

Fowler, M. J., M. J. Sullivan, B. R. Ekstrand 1973. Sleep and memory. *Science* 302-304.

Frank, J. D. 1964. Training and therapy. Chapter 16 in Bradford *et al.* (eds.) 1964.

Fries, C. C. 1947. *Teaching and Learning English as a Foreign Language*. Ann Arbor: University of Michigan Press.

Fuster, J. M. and G. E. Alexander 1971. Neuron activity related to short term memory. *Science* 652-654.

Gardner, R. C. and W. E. Lambert 1972. *Attitudes and Motivation in Second-Language Learning.* Rowley, Mass.: Newbury House.

Gartman, L. M. and N. F. Johnson 1972. Massed vs. distributed repetition of homographs: a test of the differential-encoding hypothesis. *JVLVB 11*: 801-808.

Gattegno, C. 1972. *Teaching Foreign Languages in Schools: The Silent Way.* Second edition. New York: Educational Solutions, Inc.

Gattegno, C. 1973. *The Universe of Babies.* New York: Educational Solutions, Inc.

Geen, Russell, G. 1974. Effects of evaluation apprehension on memory over intervals of varying length. *J. Exp. Psych. 102.5*:908-910.

Gibb, J. R. 1961. Defensive communication. *J. Comm. 11*:141-148.

–––. 1964. Climate for trust formation. In Bradford *et al.* (eds.).

Giffin, K. 1967. Interpersonal trust in small-group communication. *Quarterly Journal of Speech 53*:224-234.

Goldstein, K. 1963. *The Organism.* Boston: Beacon Press.

Greenburg, Dan 1965. *How to Be a Jewish Mother.* Los Angeles: Price, Stern, Sloan.

Groberg, D. 1972. *Mnemonic Japanese.* Salt Lake City: Interac.

Guiora, A. Z. 1970. Transpositional Research in the clinical process. *Compr. Psychiat. 11*:6.

–––. 1972. Construct validity and Transpositional Research: toward an empirical study of psychoanalytic concepts. *Compr. Psychiat. 13*:139-150.

Guiora, A. Z., B. Beit-Hallahmi, Robert C. L. Brannon, C. Y. Dull, T. Scovel 1972. The effects of experimentally induced changes in ego states on pronunciation ability in a second language: an exploratory study. *Compr. Psychiat. 13*:5, September: October..

Guiora, A. Z., Harlan L. Lane, L. A. Bosworth 1967. An exploration of some personality variables in authentic pronunciation of a second language. In H. Lane and E. Zale (eds.). *Studies in Language and Language Behavior.* Ann Arbor: Univ. of Michigan.

Guiora, A. Z., M. Paluszny, B. Beit-Hallahmi, J. C. Catford, R. E. Colley, and C. Y. Dull 1975. Language and person: studies in language behavior. *Language Learning 25*:43-61.

Gurowitz, E. M. 1969. *The Molecular Basis of Memory.* New York: Prentice-Hall.

Harris, Thomas A. 1967. *I'm OK-You're OK.* New York: Harper & Row.

Hawkes, John 1970. The Voice Project: an idea for innovation in the teaching of writing. In Baumbach (ed.).

Hayakawa, S. I. Conditions of success in communication. *Bull. Menninger Clinic 26*:5.

Herrigel, E. 1971. *Zen in the Art of Archery.* New York: Random House.

Hill, Jane H. 1970. Foreign accents, language acquisition, and cerebral dominance revisited. *Language Learning 20*:237-248.

Hine, B. and R. M. Paolino 1970. Retrograde anmesia: production of skeletal but not cardiac response gradient by ECS. *Science* 1224-1226.

Hogan, R. M. and W. Kintsch 1971. Differential effects of study and test trials on long-term recognition and recall. *JVLVB 10*:562-567.

Hok, R. 1972. Cognitive and S-R learning theories reconciled. *IRAL 10*:263-269.

Höweler, Marijke. 1972. Diversity of word usage as a stress indicator in an interview situation. *J. Psycholinguistic Research 1*:3 243-248.

Hydén, H. and P. W. Lange 1968. Protein synthesis in the hippocampal pyramidal cells of rats during a behavioral test. *Science* 1370-1373.

Ilfeld, F. W. and E. Lindemann 1971. Professional and community: pathways toward trust. *Am. J. Psychiatry 128*:583-589.

Jakobovits, L. A. 1970a. *Foreign Language Learning: A Psycholinguistic Analysis of the Issues.* Rowley, Mass.: Newbury House.

–––. 1970b. Prolegomena to a theory of competence. In R. C. Lugton (ed).

Jakobovits, L. A. and B. Gordon. 1974. *The Context of Foreign Language Teaching.* Rowley, Mass.: Newbury House.

Jarvik, M. E. 1970. The role of consolidation in memory. In Byrne, W. (ed.). *Molecular Approaches to Learning and Memory.* New York: Academic Press.

Jersild, Arthur T. 1955. *When Teachers Face Themselves.* New York: Teachers College Press.

Kamano, D. K. and J. E. Drew 1961. Selectivity in memory of personally significant material. *J. Gen. Psych. 65*:25-32.

Kappel, S., M. Harford, V. D. Burns, N. S. Anderson. 1975. Effects of vocalization on short-term memory for words. *J. Exp. Psych. 101*:314-317.

Katz, Robert L. 1963. *Empathy: Its Nature and Uses.* The Free Press of Glencoe.

Kintsch, W., E. J. Crothers, C. C. Jorgensen. 1971. On the role of semantic processing in short-term retention. *J. Exp. Psych. 90*:96-101.

Klein, G. S. 1956. Perception, motives and personality: a clinical perspective. In J. L. McCary (ed.) *Psychology of Personality.* New York: Grove Press.

Kleinberg, J. and H. Kaufman 1971. Constancy in STM: bits and chunks, *J. Exp. Psych. 90*:326-333.

Kleinsmith, L. J. and S. Kaplan 1963. Paired-associate learning as a function of arousal and interpolated interval. *J. Exp. Psych. 65*:190-193.

Koch, B. R. 1972. Report on an intercultural workshop in Germany. *Communique: Newsletter of Intercultural Communications Programs.*

Krashen, Stephen D. 1973. Lateralization, language, learning, and the critical period: some new evidence. *Language Learning 23*:63-74.

Krumm, H. J. 1973. Interaction analysis and microteaching for the training of modern language teachers. *IRAL 11*:163-170.

Kunihara, S. and J. J. Asher 1965. The strategy of the total physical response: an application to learning Japanese. *IRAL 3*:271-289.

Labov, W. 1966. *The Social Stratification of English in New York City.* Washington, D. C.: Center for Applied Linguistics.

Lado, R. 1965. Memory span as a factor in second language learning. *IRAL 3*:123-130.

Lado, R., T. V. Higgs, J. Edgerton 1971. *The Relationship of Thought and Memory in Linguistic Performance: 'Thought' Exercises in Foreign Language Teaching.* USOE Contract No. OEC-0-70-1626.

LaForge, Paul G. 1971. Community language learning: a pilot study. *Language Learning 21*:45-61.

–––. 1975. *Research Profiles with Community Language Learning.* Apple River, Illinois: Counseling-Learning Institutes.

Lambert, W. 1962. Psychological approaches to the study of languages. Seminar in Language and Language Learning: Final Report 63-90. Seattle: Univ. of Washington.

———. 1970. In Nelson *et al.* 1970.

Lambert W., R. C. Gardner, H. C. Barik, K. Tunstall 1963. Attitudinal and cognitive aspects of intensive study of a second language. *J. Abnormal and Social Psych.* 66:358-368.

Larson, D. N. and Wm. A. Smalley 1972. *Becoming Bilingual.* New Canaan, Connecticut: Practical Anthropology.

Levertov, Denise 1970. The untaught teacher. In Baumbach (ed.).

Lewis, M. and R. Freedle 1973. Mother-infant dyad: the cradle of meaning. In Pliner *et al.* (eds.) 127-155.

Libit, E. C. and D. R. Kent 1970. In Nelson *et al.* 1970.

Lidz, T. 1968. *The Person: His Development Throughout the Life Cycle.* New York: Basic Books.

Lipson, Alexander. 1971 Some new strategies for teaching oral skills. In Lugton (ed.) 1971. 231-244.

Loomis, J. L. 1959. Communication, the development of trust, and cooperative behavior. *Human Relations 12:*309-315.

Lott, A. J., B. E. Lott, M. L. Walsh 1970. Learning of paired associates relevant to differentially liked persons. *J. Pers. Soc. Psychol. 16:*274-283.

Lozanov, G. 1974. Information conveyed at a briefing on the use of Suggestopedia in teaching foreign languages. Ottawa.

Luborsky, L. 1971. Introduction to the fifth edition of D. Rapaport, *Emotions and Memory.* New York: International Universities Press.

Lugton, R. C. (ed.) 1971. *Toward a Cognitive Approach to Second Language Acquisition.* Philadelphia: Center for Curriculum Development.

Luria, A. R. 1968. *The Mind of a Mnemonist.* New York: Basic Books.

Lyon, H. C. 1971. *Learning to Feel—Feeling to Learn.* New York: Merrill.

Malin, D. H. and H. N. Guttman 1972. Synthetic rat scotophobin induces dark avoidance in mice. *Science* 1219-1220.

Martin, E., K. H. Roberts and A. M. Collins 1968. Short-term memory for sentences. *JVLVB* 7:560-566.

Maslow, A. H. 1970. *Motivation and Personality.* (2nd edition) New York: Harper & Row.

Mayor, S. J. 1969. Memory in the Japanese quail: effects of puromycin and acetoxycycloheximide. *Science 28:*1165-1167.

McConnell, J. V., T. Shigehisa, H. Salive 1970. Attempts to transfer approach and avoidance responses by RNA injections in rats. In Pribram & Broadbent. 129-159.

McIntosh, Lois. 1974. Calm or chaos in the classroom. *NAFSA Newsletter 26(3):*7ff.

Mehan, H. 1972. Language using abilities. *Language Sciences 22:*1-10.

Melton, A. W. 1970. The situation with respect to the spacing of repetitions and memory. *JVLVB 9:*596-606.

Metcalfe, Maryse. 1966. Problems of memory in man. In Richter (ed.) 5-14.

Miles, Matthew B. 1964. The T group and the classroom. Chapter 17 in Bradford *et al.* (eds.).

Miller, G. A. 1951. *Language and Communication.* New York: McGraw-Hill.

———. 1956. The magical number seven, plus or minus two: Some limits on our capacity for processing information. *Psychological Review 63:*81-97.

Miller, Harry 1964. *Teaching and Learning in Adult Education.* New York: Macmillan.

Milner, Brenda 1970. Memory and the medial temporal regions of the brain. In Pribram & Broadbent. 29-50.

Misanin, J. R., R. R. Miller, D. J. Lewis 1968. Retrograde amnesia produced by ECS after reactivation of a consolidated memory trace. *Science* 554-555.

Modern Language Materials Development Center 1961. *Teacher's Manual for German, Level One.* New York: Harcourt, Brace and World.

Modigliani, V. and J. G. Seamon 1974. Transfer of information from short- to long-term memory. *J. Exp. Psych. 102*:768-772.

Morray, M. K. 1975. ESL in the small college. *NAFSA Newsletter 26*:5-6.

Moskowitz, Gertrude 1968. The effects of training foreign language teachers in Interaction Analysis. *Foreign Language Annals 1*:218-235.

———. 1971. Interaction Analysis—a new modern language for supervisors. *Foreign Language Annals 5*:211-221.

———. 1974. How does *your* classroom go? *English Teaching Forum 12(2)*:26f.

Moulton, W. G. 1966. *A Linguistic Guide to Language Learning.* New York: The Modern Language Association of America.

Mueller, Theodore 1971. Could the new key be a wrong key? *The French Review 44*:6.

Nelson, R. J. *et al.* 1970. Motivation in foreign language learning. In Tursi 1970.

Nelson, T. O. 1971. Savings and forgetting from LTM. *JVLVB 10*:568-576.

Nelson, R. J., L. A. Jakobovits, F. Del Olmo, D. R. Kent, W. E. Lambert, E. C. Libit, J. W. Torrey, G. R. Tucker 1970. Motivation in Foreign Language Learning. In J.A. Tursi (ed.).

Ney, James W. 1974. Contradictions in theoretical approaches to the teaching of foreign languages. *MLJ 58*:197-200.

Nida, E. A. 1972. Sociopsychological problems in language mastery and retention. In Pimsleur, P. and T. Quinn (eds.) 1972. *The Psychology of Second Language Learning.* Cambridge.

Norman, D. A. 1970. Models of human memory. In *idem* (ed.) *Models of Human Memory.* New York: Academic Press.

Oller, J. W. 1971. Language use and foreign language learning. *IRAL 9*:161-168.

Osborn, Anne G., J. P. Bunker, L. M. Cooper, G. S. Frank, E. R. Hilgard 1967. Effects of thiopental sedation on learning and memory. *Science* 574-576.

Oskarsson, M. 1973. Assessing the relative effectiveness of two methods of teaching English to adults. *IRAL 11*:251-262.

Ott, C. E., D. C. Butler, R. S. Blake, J. P. Ball 1973. The effect of interactive-image elaboration on the acquisition of foreign language vocabulary. *Language Learning 23*:197-206.

Paolino, R. M. and H. M. Levy 1971. Amnesia produced by spreading depression and ECS: evidence for time-dependent memory-trace localization. *Science* 746-749.

Paulston, C. B. 1970. Structural pattern drills: a classification. *Foreign Language Annals 4*:187-193.

Peterson, L. R. and M. J. Peterson 1959. Short-term retention of individual items. *J. Experimental Psych. 58*:193-198.

Pinkus, A. L. and K. R. Laughery 1970. Recoding and grouping processes in STM: effects of subject-paced presentation. *J. Exp. Psych. 85*:335-341.

Pliner, Patricia, L. Krames and T. Alloway (eds.) 1973. *Communication and Affect: Language and Thought.* New York: Academic Press.

Postman, L., G. Keppel and R. Zacks 1968. Studies of learning to learn: VII. The effect of practice on response integration. *JVLVB* 7:776-784.

Prator, C. H. 1965. Development of a manipulation-communication scale. *NAFSA Studies and Papers, English Language Series* 10:385-391.

Prator, C. H. 1971. Adding a second language. In R. C. Lugton (ed.) 1971. 137-151.

Pribram, K. H. and D. E. Broadbent (eds.) 1970. *Biology of Memory.* New York: Academic Press.

Quartermain, D., B. S. McEwen, E. C. Azmitia, Jr. 1970. Amnesia produced by ECS or cycloheximide: conditions for recovery. *Science* 683-686.

Rapaport, D. A. 1971. *Emotions and Memory.* Fifth edition. New York: Internationalal Universities Press.

Rappoport, D. A. and H. F. Daginawala 1968. Changes in nuclear RNA of brain induced by olfaction in catfish. *J. Neurochem.* 15:991-1011.

Rassias, John, quoted in the *Dartmouth Alumni Magazine,* Feb. 1974.

Reber, A. S. 1967. Implicit learning of artificial grammars. *JVLVB* 6:855-863.

Reitman, W. 1970. What does it take to remember? Chapter 14 in Norman, D. A. (ed.) *Models of Human Memory.* New York: Academic Press. 469-509.

Renard, C. and C. H. Heinle, 1969. *Implementing Voix et Images de France, Part I in American Schools.* Philadelphia: Chilton Books.

Richter, Derek 1966. Biochemical aspects of memory. In *idem* (ed.) *Aspects of Learning and Memory.* New York: Basic Books.

Rivers, Wilga M. 1964. *The Psychologist and the Foreign Language Teacher.* Chicago: Univ. of Chicago.

–––. 1968. *Teaching Foreign Language Skills.* Chicago: Univ. of Chicago.

–––. 1972. Talking off the top of their heads. *TESOL Quarterly* 6:71-81.

Russell, W. R. and F. Newcombe 1966. Contributions from clinical neurology. In Richter (ed.) 15-24.

Schafer, Roy 1958. Regression in the service of the ego. In Gardner Lindzey (ed.). *Assessment of Human Motives.* New York: Holt, Rinehart & Winston.

Schneider, A. M. and W. Sherman 1968. Amnesia: a function of the temporal relation of footshock to ecs. *Science,* 12 Jan. pp. 219-221.

Schneider, Allen M., J. Tyler, D. Jinich 1974. Recovery from retrograde amnesia: a learning process. *Science* 87-88.

Seliger, H. W., S. D. Krashen, P. Ladefoged 1975. Maturational constraints in the acquisition of second language accent. *Language Sciences No. 36*:20-22.

Sheer, D. E. 1970. Electrophysiological correlates of memory consolidation. Chapter 6 in Ungar (ed.). 177-211.

Shiffrin, R. M. 1970. Memory search. Chapter 12 in Norman, D. A. (ed.) *Models of Human Memory.* 375-447.

Silberman, C. 1970. *Crisis in the Classroom.* New York: Random House.

Simon, H. A. 1974. How big is a chunk? *Science* 183:482-488.

Stevick, E. W. 1971. *Adapting and writing language lessons.* Washington, D. C.: Superintendent of Documents. (Available from TESOL, Georgetown University, Washington, D. C.)

–––. 1973. Review of Curran 1972. *Language Learning* 23:259-271.

–––. 1974. Language teaching must do an about-face. *MLJ* 58:379-384.

Strasheim, Lorraine A. 1971. "Creativity" lies trippingly on the tongue. *MLJ* 55:339-345.

Taft, R. 1954. Selective recall and memory distortion of favorable and unfavorable material. *J. Abnormal and Social Psychology* 49:23-28.

Taylor, L. L., J. C. Catford, A. Z. Guiora and H. Lane 1971. Psychological variables and the ability to pronounce a second language. *Language and Speech* 14:146-157.

Tell, P. M., and A. M. Ferguson 1974. Influence of active and passive vocalization on short-term recall. *J. Exp. Psych.* 102:347-349.

Tiger, L. 1969. *Men in Groups.* New York: Random House.

Titone, Renzo 1970. A psycholinguistic model of grammar learning and foreign language teaching. In R. C. Lugton, ed. *ESL: Current Issues.* 41-62.

Toffler, Alvin 1970. *Future Shock.* New York: Random House.

Tulving, E. 1962. The effect of alphabetical subjective organization on memorizing unrelated words. *Canadian J. of Psych.* 16:185-191.

–––. 1969. Retrograde amnesia in free recall. *Science* 89-90.

Tursi, J. A. (ed.) 1970. *Foreign Languages and the New Student.* Northeast Conference on the Teaching of Foreign Languages.

Underwood, B. J. 1969. Some correlates of item repetition in free-recall learning. *JVLVB* 8:83-94.

–––. 1970. A breakdown of the total-time law in free-recall learning. *JVLVB* 9:573-580.

Valdman, A. (ed.) 1966. *Trends in Language Teaching.* New York: McGraw-Hill.

Walker, E. L. and R. D. Tarte 1963. Memory storage as a function of arousal and time with homogeneous and heterogeneous lists. *JVLVB* 2:113-119.

Wardhaugh, R. 1971. Teaching English to speakers of other languages: the state of the art. In R. C. Lugton (ed.) *Toward a Cognitive Approach to Second Language Acquisition.* 7-29.

Wilson, V. and B. Wattenmaker 1973. *Relevant, Enjoyable and Live Communication in Foreign Language.* Unpublished.

Zaleznik, A. and D. Moment 1964. *The Dynamics of Interpersonal Behavior.* New York: Wiley.

Index

ABEL, E. L.   21
Acceptance   83, 95, 152
Achievement   *See* Motivation
"Activity"   *See* Transactional Analysis
Adapted Child   *See* Transactional Analysis, ego-states
Adult   *See* Transactional Analysis, ego-states
Affect   36, 55, 59, 114
Alienation   113f
ALLPORT, G.   23
ANISFELD, M.   18
"Anomie"   48
ANTHONY, E. M.   105, 123
Anxiety   86, 90, 115, 153
Applied linguistics   52, 152f
Approval   *See* Motivation
Arousal   *See* Memory
ASHER, J. J.   37, 138
Association   *See* Memory
ATKINSON, R. C. and R. M. SHIFFRIN   19

Audiolingualism   17, 104, 109, 114, 121, 154f
AUSUBEL, D.   113
Authority, patterns of   91f, 158

BACHMAN, J. G.   92
BACKUS, O.   125
BANCROFT, W. J.   155
BARONDES, S. H.   8
BARONDES, S. H. and H. D. COHEN   7
BEGIN, Y.   83, 126
Belonging   *See* Hierarchy of needs
BENNE, K. D. *et al.*   95
BENNIS, W.   91
BENSON, D. F. and N. GESCHWIND   27
BERNE, E.   Chapter V, 86, 103, 120, 137f, 142
BEVER, T. G. and R. J. CHIARELLO   16
BJORK, E.   26, 28
BLUBAUGH, J. A.   63

BLUMENTHAL, A. L.   10
BOGOCH, S.   10
BORDEN, R. C. and A. C. BUSSE   93
BOSCO, F. J. and DI PIETRO, R. J.
108f, 114
BOWER, G. H. and D. WINZENZ   26,
32
BRADFORD, L. P. *et al.*   94
BRAUD, W. G.   5
BRIERLY, J. B.   27, 38
BROWN, M.   77
BRUNER, J.   40f, 51, 110
BUGELSKI, B. R.   20
BUSCHKE, H.   143

CARROLL, J. B.   12, 15
Catfish   5
CERASO, J.   29, 32
CHAFE, W. L.   7, 27, 30
CHASTAIN, K.   97, 104, 114, 120
Chemical aspects of memory   *See*
Memory
Chess   17
Child   *See* Transactional Analysis,
ego-states
Choices made by learner   117, 144
Chunking   *See* Memory
CICCONE, D. S.   28
Cognitive aspects of memory   *See*
Memory
"Cognitive code"   104, 109, 114, 121,
140
Cognitive depth   *See* Memory
COLES, R.   33
Communication   33, 43, 124
"fact-fict" type of "communica-
tion"   34, 43
Community   98f, 114, 126, 141, 147,
152, 159
Community Language Learning   116,
Chapter VIII, 143, 146, 157
Confidence, role of   147, 156, 160
Consolidation of memories   *See*
Memory
Controlling function of Parent   *See*
Transactional Analysis, ego-states
"Coping"   41
Counseling-Learning   133, 158

Correction   *See* Errors
"Counseling response"   97
CRAIK, F.   27, 30ff, 35, 36, 139
Creativity   151f, 156, 160
CREDIF   *See* Saint-Cloud
Crowding   *See* Memory
Cuisenaire rods   *See* Rods
CURRAN, C. A.   19, 27, 32, 40ff,
50, 66, 80, 83, 86, 94f, 97f, 106,
110, 114, 120, 123, Chapter VIII,
136f, 143

DARLEY, C. F. and B. M. MURDOCK
15, 79
Dealienation   *See* Alienation
DEESE, J.   23
Defensiveness on part of learner   40,
61f, 75, 90, 109f, 112, 115, 120,
147, 150, 154, 158
Depth   30, 34f, 43, 93, 98, 109,
116, 118f, 124, 150
Depth, cognitive   *See* Memory
DEUTSCH, D.   12
DEUTSCH, J. A.   8, 9
DILLER, K.   80
Direct Method   109, 114
Distributed practice   *See* Memory,
time
"Doubleplaneness"   158
Drills   35, Chapter V, 76, 116
Drugs   *See* Memory

EARHARD, M.   21
EBBINGHAUS   29
Ego-states   *See* Transactional Analysis
Electrical aspects of memory   *See*
Memory
ELLIOTT, G.   99, 113
ELLIS, F. R. *et al.*   41
Emotional factors   9, 27, 36, 38, 41,
59, 67, 78, 93, 146, 155
Empathy   54
Errors, correction of   142, 155
ERVIN, F. R. and T. ANDREWS   10,
26
Esteem   *See* Hierarchy of needs
Exercises   81ff, 117
Extrinsic motivation   *See* Motivation

"Fact-fict"   *See* Communication
Fear   86
Flashcards   18
Flatworms   5
Fluency   59ff
FOWLER, M. J. *et al.*   27
Fraenum fork   93
FRANK, J. D.   97
Free recall   *See* Memory, recall
FRIES, C. C.   138
FUSTER, J. M. and G. E. ALEXANDER.
    4

GAGLIARDO, M.   145
Games   *See* Transactional Analysis
GARDNER, R. C. and W. E. LAMBERT
    111, 113
GARTMAN, L. M. and N. F. JOHNSON
    28
GATTEGNO, C.   69, 120f, Chapter
    IX
GEEN, R. G.   40
Generative aspects of memory   *See*
    Memory
GIBB, J. R.   91, 95, 99
GIFFIN, K.   95f
Goldfish   5
GOLDSTEIN, K.   80
Grammar-Translation Method   109,
    114
GREENBURG, D.   67
GROBERG, D.   20
Group relationships   Chapter VI,
    141
GUIORA, A. *et al.*   54ff
GUROWITZ, E. M.   4, 5

HARRIS, T. A.   23, Chapter V, 103,
    106, 137
HAWKES, J.   99
HAYAKAWA, S. I.   86
HERRIGEL, E.   146
Hierarchy of needs   49f, 98
    "belonging," need for   50, 52,
        83, 151, 153
    esteem, need for   50, 98, 150,
        153
    security of learner   52, 94, 97f,

126, 137, 146, 150, 152f, 155,
    159
"self-actualization"   50, 120, 151
HILL, J. H.   55
HINE, B. and R. M. PAOLINO   9
HOGAN, R. M. and W. KINTSCH   23
HOK, R.   104
Holistic   *See* Pronunciation
HÖWELER, M.   63
HYDÉN, H. *et al.*   4, 5
"Hypermnesia"   42

Identity   59, 61
ILFELD, F. W. and E. LINDEMAN
    91
Images   *See* Memory
"Infantilisation"   43, 156
Inner criteria   23, 24, 140, 147
Instrumental motivation   *See* Motivation
Integrative motivation   *See* Motivation
Interaction Analysis   91, 122
Intrinsic motivation   *See* Motivation
"Investment" on the part of the learner   25, 40, 42, 126, 151, 158
    159

JAKOBOVITS, L. A.   12, 48, 60,
    108
JAKOBOVITS, L. and B. GORDON
    91, 106, 128, 130f
JARVIK, M. E.   7
JERSILD, A. T.   96ff, 90f, 95
JORDEN, E. H.   118

KAMANO, D. K. and J. E. DREW
    39
KAPPEL, S. M. *et al.*   31, 35
KINTSCH, W. *et al.*   25, 32
KLEIN, G. S.   37
KLEINBERG, J. and H. KAUFMAN
    17
KLEINSMITH, L. J. and S. KAPLAN
    39
KOCH, B. R.   96
KRASHEN, S.   55
KRUMM, H. J.   91, 122

KUNIHARA, S. and J. ASHER   37, 138

LABOV, W.   52
LADO, R.   12, 17
LA FORGE, P.   83, 92f, 94, 126, 132, 143
LAMBERT, W.   38, 48, 60, 92, 98, 111
Language ego   54
LARSON, D. N. and W. A. SMALLEY   113
Lathophobic aphasia   78
Learner, control by   26, 29
LEVERTOV, D.   96, 99, 140f, 143
LEWIS, M. and R. FREEDLE   120
"Liberated Spanish"   82
LIBIT, E. C. and D. R. KENT   98, 121
Linguistic analysis   122
Linguistics, applied   See Applied linguistics
LIPSON, A.   108
Long-term memory   See Memory
LOOMIS, J. L.   99
LOTT, A. J., B. E. LOTT and M. L. WALSH   38
LOZANOV, G.   41ff, 44, 120, 155f
LUBORSKY, L.   41
LURIA, A. R.   21f
LYON, H. C.   75, 85, 87, 90

MALIN, D. H. and H. N. GUTTMAN   5
Marijuana   See Memory, drugs
MARTIN, E. et al.   23
MASLOW, A.   50ff, 83, 90, 103, 120, 137
Massed practice   See Memory, time
MAYOR, S. J.   139
MC CONNELL, J. V. et al.   5
MC INTOSH, L.   152f
Meaning, psychological   48, 51, 65ff, 125
Meaning, role in memory   See Memory
Mediators   See Memory
MEHAN, H.   108
MELTON, A. W.   28

Memory
  "arousal"   40f
  associations in   18, 22, 29
  chemical aspects of   5
  chunking   16
  cognitive aspects of learning   25, 112
  cognitive depth   30, 32
  consolidation of   6f
  "crowding" in   22, 28f, 77
  drugs as factors in   21, 29
  effects of voicing on   31
  electrical aspects of   4f, 27, 39
  free recall   13, 79
  generative aspects of   23
  images in   18, 22, 28, 76, 79
  long-term   7, 12, 21, 26, 35, 77
  meaning, role of   27, 35
  mediators in   19, 25f
  for pairs of items   18
  physical aspects of   4
  primacy effect   14, 21
  primary   26, 31
  processing of   30f, 139
  recall   23, 25, 29
  recency effect   13, 31
  recognition   25, 29
  for relationships   15, 79
  secondary   26
  "security words" in   19
  sensory register   26
  sleep   27
  short-term   7, 12, 21, 25f, 76, 139, 143
  subjective organizing in   20f
  tertiary   26
  time as a factor in   8, 12, 26, 143
    distributed practice   28, 77
    massed practice   28, 77
    pacing of study   28
    spacing of learning   28
  transfer of   5
  "worktable" in   20f, 41
METCALFE, M.   27
MILES, M. B.   85, 90, 94
MILLER, G. A.   16, 27
MILLER, H.   95
MILNER, B.   7
MISANIN, J. R. et al.   9

MODIGLIANI, V. and J. G. SEAMON
    26
Monkeys   2
MORRAY, M. K.   152
MOSKOWITZ, G.   91, 122
Motivation   48, 97f, 114, 158
    achievement as a source of   151,
    155
    approval as a source of   142, 152f
    "extrinsic"   49
    "instrumental"   48, 60, 92, 110
    "integrative"   48, 53, 60, 92, 110
    "intrinsic"   49
MOULTON, W. G.   59
MUELLER, T.   104

Natural Child   See Transactional
    Analysis, ego-states
"Natural" functions of Parent   See
    Transactional Analysis, ego-states
Negative recency   See Memory,
    recency
NELSON, R. J.   29, 99, 139
NEWMARK, L.   113
NEY, J. W.   104
NIDA, E. A.   60f
Nonverbal behavior   42, 120, 149
NORMAN, D. A.   139

O'CONNELL, P.   155f
OK vs. NOT-OK position   See Trans-
    actional Analysis
OLLER, J. W.   30
OSBORN, A. G. et al.   21
OSKARSSON, M.   104
OTT, C. E. et al.   20, 32

Pacing of study   See Memory, time
Pairs of items, memory for   See Mem-
    ory
PAOLINO, R. M. and H. M. LEVY   4
Parent   See Transactional Analysis,
    ego-states
Pastimes   See Transactional Analysis
PETERSON, L. R. and M. J. PETERSON
    12
Physical aspects of memory   See
    Memory

PINKUS, A. L. and K. R. LAUGHERY
    29
POSTMAN, L. et al.   26
Power   91f
PRATOR, C. H.   122
Primacy effect   See Memory
Primary memory   See Memory
Processing of memories   See Memory
Productive   68, 75, 77, 107, 116,
    119, 122, 123, 154
Pronunciation   Chapter IV, 51ff
    "analytical" view of   52
    "holistic" view of   52
    "Psychodynamic"   191ff, 122

QUARTERMAIN, D. et al.   4, 9

RAPAPORT, D. A.   41
RAPPOPORT, D. A. and H. F. DAGIN-
    AWALA   5
RASSIAS, J.   17
Rats   4, 8
Reality-testing   94, 112, 123
REBER, A. S.   15
Recall   See Memory
Recency effect   See Memory
Receptivity   56, 68, 75, 109, 111,
    114, 119, 123
Recognition   See Memory
Reflective   75, 77, 107, 122f, 151,
    154
"Reflective" phase of Community
    Language Learning   126
Regression in service of the ego   43,
    55f
REITMAN, W.   15
Relationships, memory for   See
    Memory
RENARD, C. and C. H. HEINLE
    149ff
Response by learner   38
RICHTER, D.   6, 38
Rituals   See Transactional Analysis
RIVERS, W. M.   49, 53, 78, 98, 108,
    113, 117
Rods   138ff, 145
ROGERS, C.   86, 92
Roles of teacher   See Teacher

RUSSELL, W. R. and F. NEWCOMBE
7, 27

Saint-Cloud Method   149f
SAUER, K.   82
SCHAFER, R.   43, 55
"Schlemiel"   See Transactional
Analysis, games
SCHNEIDER, A. M. et al.   10
SCHNEIDER, A. M. and W. SHERMAN
9
Secondary memory   See Memory
Security   See Hierarchy of needs
"Security words" in memory   See
Memory
Self-actualization   See Hierarchy of
needs
Self concept   55, 61, 86
SELIGER, H. W. et al.   34, 53
Sensory register   See Memory
SHEER, D. E.   6
SHIFFRIN, R. N.   18, 29
Short-term memory   See Memory
SILBERMAN, C.   85
Silent Way (The)   17, 24, Chapter
IX, 157
SIMON, H. A.   17
Simultaneous interpreters   13, 35f
Sleep   See Memory
SOMMER, M.   130
Spacing of study   See Memory, time
STRASHEIM, L.   119
Strokes   See Transactional Analysis
"Stupid"   See Transactional Anal-
ysis, games
Subjective organizing in memory
See Memory
Suggestology and Suggestopedia   42f,
155f
Synesthesia   22

TAFT, R.   40
TAYLOR, L. L. et al.   54ff
"Teach, then test"   122f, 144, 154
Teacher   Chapter VI, 85, 130, 159f
TELL, P. M. and A. M. FERGUSON
31
Tension   146

Tertiary memory   See Memory
TIGER, L.   52
TITONE, R.   108, 140
TOFFLER, A.   52
"Total Physical Response"   37f
TRANEL, D.   126
Transactional Analysis   66ff, 79, 96,
106, 123, 132, 142
activity   70
ego-states   66, 78
"adapted" Child   68, 75, 77f,
123
Adult   68f, 79f, 91, 96, 106,
132, 137, 142
Child   67, 79, 83, 88f, 132,
142, 152, 156
"controlling" functions of Parent
67, 75, 78, 123
"natural" Child   68
"natural" functions of Parent
67, 123
Parent   66f, 80, 86, 89, 106,
132, 138, 142, 152
games (in TA sense)   71, 86f, 90
"Schlemiel"   73
"Stupid"   74
"Why Don't You–Yes, But"
71
OK vs. NOT-OK position   68, 73,
79, 86, 88
pastimes   71, 81, 117
ritual   70, 81
"strokes"   69, 82, 89
transactions   66, 69
Transfer of memory   See Memory
Trust   95f, 98, 119
TULVING, E.   21, 41
TURSI, J. A.   98

UNDERWOOD, B. J.   28

"Voice in community"   98
Voicing, effects on memory   See
Memory

WALKER, E. L. and R. D. TARTE
41
WARDHAUGH, R.   108, 121

WATKINS   25
Whole-person learning   42, 150
"Why Don't You—Yes, But"   *See*
    Transactional Analysis, games
WILSON, V. and B. WATTENMAKER
    81, 98, 119
"Worktable"   *See* Memory

ZALEZNIK, A. and D. MOMENT
    91ff